THREE WAYS OF LOVING GOD

Three Ways Of
Loving God

ST. AUGUSTINE
ST. TERESA OF AVILA
ST. FRANCIS DE SALES

PARACLETE PRESS
BREWSTER, MASSACHUSETTS

2014 First printing

Three Ways of Loving God

The portions of this text taken from *The Confessions of St. Augustine*, including biographical material and notes, are copyright © 2014 by The Community of Jesus, Inc.

The portions of this text taken from St. Teresa of Avila's *The Way of Perfection*, plus biographical material about the author, are copyright © 2014 by Paraclete Press, Inc.

The portions of this text taken from St. Francis de Sales's *Treatise on the Love of God*, plus biographical material about the author, are copyright © 2014 by Bernard Bangley.

ISBN 978-1-61261-499-1

Consists of excerpts from material previously published by Paraclete Press, Inc.

In the portion taken from *Treatise on the Love of God*:

All Scripture quotations, unless otherwise indicated, are taken from the Holy Bible, New International Version®, NIV®. Copyright © 1973, 1978, 1984 by Biblica, Inc.™ Used by permission of Zondervan. All rights reserved worldwide.

Scripture quotations marked (NRSV) are taken from the Holy Bible, New Revised Standard Version, copyright © 1989, 1995 by the Division of Christian Education of the National Council of the Churches of Christ in the United States of America, and are used by permission. All rights reserved.

Scripture quotations marked (TEV) are taken from Today's English Version, Second Edition, Copyright © 1966, 1971, 1976, 1992 American Bible Society. Used by permission.

The Paraclete Press name and logo (dove on cross) are trademarks of Paraclete Press, Inc.

Cover Art by Sharon France. Sharon's original paintings can be found at: www.francegallery.net

Library of Congress Cataloging-in-Publication Data is available.

10 9 8 7 6 5 4 3 2 1

Published by Paraclete Press
Brewster, Massachusetts
www.paracletepress.com

Printed in the United States of America

CONTENTS

FOREWORD

This is a deceptively simple book, written by three experts on the Christian spiritual life. Each of them writes with clarity, and from a great depth of personal experience, and yet what they describe is something that is ultimately beyond description. That's what we mean when we say the book is deceptively simple: you cannot obtain what they describe by simply reading.

This is a collection of three distinct but united voices on the subject of what it means to love God, and to know that you are loved by God. In these pages, you will meet three of the most interesting Christians in the history of our faith: St. Augustine of Hippo, St. Teresa of Avila, and St. Francis de Sales. Their viewpoints are presented chronologically. Short biographies of each may be found at the conclusion of the book.

ST. AUGUSTINE

From *The Confessions*

BOOK X
The Examined Life

ONE

Let me know you, Lord, who know me;[1] *let me know you even as I am known*. O Strength of my soul, enter it and make it fit for you, that you may enjoy it *without spot or wrinkle*. This is my hope; therefore I speak, and in this hope I rejoice when I rightly rejoice. The less other things of this life deserve our sorrow, the more we weep for them; and the more they ought to be sorrowed for, the less men weep for them. For behold, you love truth and *he who knows the truth comes to the light*. This I would do in my heart before you in this confession and in my writing before many witnesses.

TWO

What is there in me that could be hidden from you, O Lord, to whose eyes the depths of man's conscience is bare, even though I did not confess it? I might hide you from myself, but not myself from you. But now my groanings bear witness that I am displeased with myself and that you shine brightly and are pleasing, beloved and desired. I am ashamed of myself and renounce myself, and choose you, for I can neither please you nor myself except in you. Therefore I am open to you, Lord, with all that I am, and whatever benefit may come from my confession to you, I have spoken. I do not confess merely with words and fleshly sounds, but with the words of my soul and the cry of my thoughts which your ear knows. For when I am wicked, confession to you is nothing more than to be displeased with myself. But when I am truly devout, it is to ascribe glory to you; because you, Lord, bless the godly, but first you *justify him who is ungodly*.[2] My confession then, O my God, is made both silently and yet not silently, for in sound it is silent, but in affection, it cries aloud. For I neither utter any right thing to others which you have not already heard from me, nor do you hear any such things from me which you have not first said to me.

THREE

But what do I have to do with men that they should hear my confessions, as if they could heal all my infirmities? They are a race, curious to know the lives of others, slow to amend their own. Why do they seek to hear from me what I am, who will not hear from you what they themselves are? And how do they know, when from me they hear of myself, whether I speak the truth, since *no man knows what is in man, but the spirit of man which is in him*? But if they hear from you about themselves, they cannot say, "The Lord lies." For what is it to hear from you of themselves, but to know themselves? And who knows and says, "It is false," unless he lies to himself? But because *charity believes all things*—at least among those whom it knits together with itself as one—I, too, Lord, will confess to you in such a way that men may hear, though I cannot prove to them that my confession is true; yet those whose ears are opened to me by charity will believe me.

But, O my inmost Physician, make plain to me what benefit I may gain by doing it. You have forgiven and covered my past sins that you might make me happy in you, changing my soul by faith and your sacrament. When my confessions of them are read and heard, they stir up the heart. No longer does it sleep in despair and say, "I cannot," but it awakes in the love of your mercy and the sweetness of your grace, by which whoever is weak is made strong, when he becomes conscious of his own weakness by it. And the good delight to hear of the past evils of those who are now freed from them—not because they are evils, but because they were and no longer are.

What does it profit me, O Lord my God, what does this book gain me, to confess to men in your presence what I now am? My conscience confesses daily to you, trusting more in the hope of your mercy than in its own innocence. For I have seen and spoken of the fruit of knowing what I have been, but what I now am, at the very time of making these confessions, various people want to know, both those who have known me and those who have not, who have heard from me or of me. But their ear is not at my heart, where I am whatever I am. They wish to hear me confess what I am within, where neither their eye, nor ear, nor understanding can read. They wish it and are ready to believe it—but will they know? For charity, which makes them good, tells them that I do not lie in my confessions, and charity in them believes me.

FOUR

But for what good purpose do they wish to hear this? Do they want to rejoice with me when they hear how near by your grace I approach to you? Do they wish to pray for me when they hear how much I am held back by my own weight? To such I will disclose myself.[3] For it is no little gain, O Lord my God, that thanks should be given to you on our behalf, and that you should be entreated for us. Let the brotherly soul love in me what you teach is to be loved, and lament in me what you teach is to be lamented. Let it be a brotherly, not an alien soul—not one of those strange children, *whose mouth speaks vanity, and whose right hand is the hand of falsehood.* But let it be the soul of my brethren who, when they approve, rejoice for me, and when they disapprove, are sorry for me; because whether they approve or disapprove, they love me. To such I will disclose myself; they will breathe freely at my good deeds, sigh for my ill. My good deeds are your appointments and your gifts. My evil ones are my offenses and your judgments. Let them breathe freely at the one and sigh at the other. Let hymns and weeping go up into your sight from the hearts of my brethren, your censers.[4] And be pleased, O Lord, with the incense of your holy temple; *have mercy on me according to your great mercy* for your own name's sake. And do not on any account leave what you have begun in me, but perfect my imperfections.

This is the fruit, the profit of my confession of what I am, not of what I have been: to confess this, not only before you, in a secret exultation with trembling, and a secret sorrow with hope, but in the ears of the believing sons of men, sharers of my joy, partners in my mortality, my fellow citizens and fellow pilgrims, who have gone before me, and are to follow on—companions of my way. These are your servants, my brethren, who are your sons by your will. They are my masters, whom you command me to serve if I would live with you and in you. But this, your Word, would mean little to me if it only commanded by speaking, without going before in action. This then I do in deed and word. This I do under your wings, for it would be too great a peril if my soul were not subjected to you under your wings and my infirmities known to you. I am but a little one, but my Father ever lives, and my Guardian is sufficient for me. For he is the same who gave me life and defends me, and you yourself are all my good. You, Almighty One, are with me, yes, even before I am with you. To those then whom you command me to serve I will show, not what I have been, but what I now am, and what I continue to be. But I do not judge myself. Thus, therefore would I be heard.

FIVE

You, Lord, are my Judge, because, although *no man knows the things of a man but the spirit of a man that is in him*, yet there is something of man that *the spirit of man that is in him*, itself, does not know. But you, Lord, know him completely, for you made him. And although I despise myself in your sight and account myself *dust and ashes*, I know something of you that I do not know of myself. Truly, *now we see through a glass darkly*, not *face to face* as yet. As long, then, as I am absent from you, I am more present with myself than with you. And I know that you cannot be violated, but I do not know which temptations I can resist and which I cannot. There is hope, because you are faithful, *who will not allow us to be tempted beyond our ability; but will with the temptation also make a way of escape, so that we may be able to bear it.* I will confess then what I know of myself; I will confess also what I do not know of myself. What I know of myself I know by your light shining upon me; and what I do not know of myself, I continue not to know until my *darkness becomes as the noonday* in the light of your countenance.

SIX

Ilove you, Lord, without any doubt, but with assured certainty.
You have stricken my heart with your Word, and I love you.
Yes, also, heaven and earth and all that is in them on every side
bid me to love you. They will not cease to say so to everyone, so
that *they are without excuse*. But more profoundly, *you will have
mercy on whom you will have mercy, and compassion on whom you
will have compassion*. Otherwise, the heaven and the earth speak
your praises to deaf ears.

But what do I love when I love you? Not the beauty of bodies,
nor the fair harmony of time, nor the brightness of the light, so
gladsome to our eyes; not the sweet melodies of various songs,
nor the fragrant smell of flowers and ointments and spices;
not manna and honey; not the limbs that physical love likes to
embrace. It is none of these that I love when I love my God.
Yet I love a kind of light, a kind of melody, a kind of fragrance,
a kind of food, and a kind of embrace when I love my God:
the light, the melody, the fragrance, the food, and the embrace
of the inner man, where there shines into my soul what space
cannot contain, and there sounds what time cannot carry away.
I breathe a fragrance that no breeze scatters, and I taste there
what is not consumed by eating; and there I lie in the embrace
that no satiety can ever separate. This is what I love when I love
my God.

And what is it? I asked the earth, and it answered me, "I am
not he." And whatever is in the earth confessed the same. I asked
the sea and its deeps, and the living, creeping things, and they
answered, "We are not your God; seek him above us." I asked
the moving air; and the whole air with its inhabitants answered,
"Anaximenes was deceived; I am not God."[5] I asked the heavens,
sun, moon, stars. "No," say they, "we are not the God whom you
seek." And I replied to all the things that throng about the senses

of my flesh, "You have told me of my God, that you are not he. Tell me something of him." And they cried, "He made us." My questioning of them was my thoughts about them, and their form of beauty gave the answer. And I turned myself to myself, and said to myself, "What are you?" And I answer, "A man." And behold, in me there appear both soul and body, one outside and the other within. By which of these should I seek my God? I had sought him in the body from earth to heaven, as far as I could send my eyesight as messengers. But the better part is the inner, for to it, as to a ruler and judge, all the bodily messengers reported the answers of heaven and earth and all things in them, who said, "We are not God, but he made us." These things my inner man knew by means of the outer. I, the inner man, knew them. I, the mind, knew them through the senses of my body. I asked the whole frame of the world about my God; and it answered me, "I am not he, but he made me."

Is not this outward appearance visible to all who have use of their senses? Why then does it not say the same thing to all? Animals small and great see it, but they cannot ask it anything, because their senses are not endowed with reason, so they cannot judge what they see. But men can ask, *so that the invisible things of God may be clearly seen, being understood by the things that are made*. But in loving them, they are brought into subjection to them, and subjects cannot judge.[6] Nor do these things answer unless the questioners can judge. The creatures do not change their voice, they do not appear one way to this man, another to that; but appearing the same way to both, they are dumb to one and speak to the other. Rather, they speak to all, but only those understand who compare the voice received externally with the internal truth. For truth says to me, "Neither heaven nor earth nor any other body is your God." This, their very nature says to him who sees them, "They are a mass; a mass is less in part than in the whole." Now I speak to you, O my soul; you are my better part, for you quicken the whole mass of my body, giving it life. No body can give life to a body. But your God is the Life of your life.

SEVEN

What do I do, then, when I love my God? Who is he who is so high above my soul? By my very soul I will ascend to him. I will soar beyond that power by which I am united to my body, filling its whole frame with life. But I do not find God by that power, for then, so could *horse and mule that have no understanding* find him, for it is the same power by which their bodies live.[7] But there is another power, not only that by which I am made alive, but that, too, by which I imbue my flesh with sense, which the Lord has made for me, commanding the eye not to hear and the ear not to see; but commanding the eye that I should see through it, and the ear that I should hear through it, and the several other senses, what is to each their own proper places and functions. Through these different senses, I, as a single mind, act. I will go beyond this power of mine, too, for the horse and mule also have this power, for they also perceive through their bodily senses.

EIGHT

I will move on, then, beyond this power of my nature, rising by degrees to him who made me. And I come to the fields and spacious palaces of my memory, where the treasures of innumerable images are stored, brought there from all sorts of things perceived by the senses. Further, there is stored up in memory whatever thoughts we think, either by enlarging or diminishing, or changing in any other way those things that the senses have brought in; and whatever else has been committed and stored up, which forgetfulness has not yet swallowed up and buried. When I enter there, I ask what I want brought forth, and some things appear instantly; others must be sought after longer, and are brought, as it were, out of some inner storage place. Still others rush out in crowds, and while only one thing is desired and asked for, they leap into view as if to say, "Do you perhaps want me?" I drive these away from the face of my remembrance with the hand of my heart until what I wanted is unveiled and appears in sight out of its secret place. Other things come up readily, in unbroken order, as they are called for—those in front giving way to those that follow; and as they make way, they are hidden from sight, ready to come back at my will. All of this takes place when I repeat something by heart.

And all these things are preserved distinctly and under general heads, each having entered my memory by its own particular avenue: light and colors and forms of bodies, by the eyes; all sorts of sounds by the ears; all smells by the avenue of the nostrils; all tastes by the mouth; and by the sensation of the whole body, what is hard or soft, hot or cold, smooth or rugged, heavy or light—either external or internal to the body. All these things the great recesses, the hidden and unknown caverns of memory, receive and store, to be retrieved and brought forth when needed, each entering by its own gate. Yet the things themselves do not enter, but only the images of the things perceived are there, ready to be recalled in thought. But how these images are formed, who can tell? It is plain, however, which sense brought each one in and stored it up. For even while I dwell in darkness and silence, I can produce colors in my memory if I choose, and I can discern between black and white. Sounds do not break in and alter the image brought in by my eyes which I am reviewing, though they also are there, lying dormant and stored, as it were, separately. I can call for these, too, and they immediately appear. And though my voice is still and my throat silent, I can sing as much as I will. Those images of colors do not intrude, even though they are there, when another memory is called for which came in by way of the ears. So it is with other things brought in and stored up by the other senses—I can recall them at my pleasure. Yes, I can tell the fragrance of lilies from violets, though I smell nothing; I prefer honey to sweet wine, smooth surfaces to rough ones—at the time neither tasting nor handling, but only remembering.

These things I do inside myself, in that vast hall of my memory. For present there with me are heaven, earth, sea, and whatever I could think on them, in addition to what I have forgotten. There also I meet with myself, and recall myself—what, when, and where I did a thing, and what my feelings were when I did it. All that I remember is there, either personal experiences or what I was told by others. Out of the same store I continually combine with the past fresh images of things experienced, or what I have believed from what I have experienced. From these I can project future actions, events, and hopes, and I can reflect on all these again in the present. I say to myself, in that great storehouse of my mind, filled with the images of so many and such great things, "I will do this or that, and this or that will follow." "Oh, would that this or that might be!" "May God prevent this or that!" This is the way I talk to myself, and when I speak, the images of all I speak about are present, out of the same treasury of memory. I could not say anything at all about them if their images were not there.

Great is this power of memory, exceedingly great, O my God: a large and boundless chamber! Who has ever sounded the depths of it? Yet this is a power of mine, and it belongs to my nature. But I do not myself comprehend all that I am. Therefore the mind is too narrow to contain itself. But where can that part be which it does not itself contain? Is it outside it and not inside? How then does it not comprehend itself? A great wonder arises in me; I am stunned with amazement at this. And men go outside themselves to admire the heights of mountains, the mighty waves of the sea, the broad tides of rivers, the width of the ocean and the circuits of the stars, passing by themselves. They do not wonder at the fact that when I spoke of all these things, I did not see them with my eyes, yet I could not have spoken of them unless I then inwardly saw with my memory the mountains, waves, rivers, and stars that I have seen, and that ocean that I believe to exist, and with the same vast spaces between them as if I saw them outside myself. Yet I did not actually draw them into myself by seeing them, when I beheld them with my eyes, but only their images. And I know which sense of the body impressed each of them on me.

NINE

Yet these are not all that the immeasurable capacity of my memory retains. Here also is all that I have learned of the liberal sciences and have not yet forgotten—removed as it were to some inner place, which is yet no place. In this case it is not the images that are retained, but rather, the things themselves. For whatever literature, whatever art of debating, however many kinds of questions I know, they exist in my memory as they are—I have not taken in their image and left out the thing itself. It is not as though it had sounded and passed away like a voice retained in the ear, which can be recalled as if it still sounded when it no longer sounded. Nor is it like an odor that evaporates into the air as it passed, affecting the sense of smell, and from it carries an image of itself into the memory that we renew when we recall it. Nor is it like food, which verily has no taste in the belly, but yet is still tasted in some way in the memory; nor as anything that the body feels by touch and that the memory still conceives when removed from us. For those things themselves are not transmitted into the memory, but their images are caught up and stored, with an admirable swiftness, as it were, in wonderful cabinets, and from there wonderfully brought forth by the act of remembering.

TEN

But now when I hear that there are three kinds of questions—whether a thing is, what it is, of what kind it is—I do indeed hold the images of the sounds that make up these words, and I know that those sounds passed through the air with a noise and then ceased to be. But the questions themselves that are conveyed by these sounds, I never reached with any sense of my body, nor do I ever see them at all except by my mind. Yet I have not laid up their images in my memory, but these very questions themselves. How they entered into me, let them say if they can; for I have gone over all the avenues of my flesh, and cannot find how they entered. For the eyes say, "If those images were colored, we reported about them." The ears say, "If they made a sound, we gave you knowledge of them." The nostrils say, "If they have any smell, they passed by us." The taste says, "Unless they have a flavor, do not ask me." The touch says, "If it has no size, I did not handle it, and if I did not handle it, I have no account of it."

How and from where did these things enter my memory? I do not know. For when I learned them, I gave no credit to another man's mind, but recognized them in mine; and approving them as true, I commended them to my mind, laying them up as it were, where I could get at them again whenever I wished. There they were then [in my mind] before I stored them in my memory. Where then, or why, when they were spoken, did I acknowledge them and say, "So it is! It is true," unless they were already in the memory, but so thrown back and buried as it were in deeper recesses, that if the suggestion of another had not drawn them forth, I may have been unable to conceive of them?[8]

ELEVEN

Thus we find that to learn those things whose images do not come to us by way of the senses, but which we know by themselves as they are, without images, is nothing more than taking the things the memory already has—scattered and unarranged. By marking and careful attention we gather them, as it were in that same memory where they lay unknown before scattered and ignored, so that they can readily occur to the mind now familiarized with them. And how many things of this kind does my memory hold that have already been discovered, and, as I said, placed as it were handily, which we are said to have learned and come to know? And if I for some short space should cease to call them back to mind, they would again be so buried, and glide back, as it were, into the deeper recesses, that they would have to be drawn out again as if new from the same place. For there is nowhere else for them to go, but they must be drawn together again that they may be known. That is to say, they must be collected together from their scattering. From this the word *to cogitate* comes. For *cogo* [I collect] and *cogito* [I re-collect] have the same relation to each other as *ago* [I do] and *agito* [I do frequently], *facio* [I make] and *facito* [I make frequently]. But the mind has appropriated to itself this word, *cogito*, so that, not what is collected anywhere, but only what is re-collected, that is, brought together in the mind, is properly said to be cogitated or thought upon.

TWELVE

The memory also contains innumerable principles and laws of numbers and dimensions, none of which have been impressed upon it by any bodily sense, since they have neither color, sound, taste, smell, nor touch. I have heard the sound of the words by which they are signified, but the sounds are other than the things themselves. For the sounds are different in Greek than in Latin, but the things are neither Greek nor Latin, nor any other language. I have seen the lines of architects, the very finest, like a spider's thread; but the truths they express are not the images of those lines, which my physical eye saw. The architect knows them without any use whatsoever of a body, by recognizing them within himself. I have perceived, also, with all the senses of my body the numbers of the things that we count, but those numbers themselves by which we count are different. They are not the images of the things we count, and therefore they simply *are*. Let him who does not see these truths laugh at me for saying them. While he derides me, I will pity him.

THIRTEEN

I hold all these things in my memory, and I remember how I learned them. I remember, too, having heard many things erroneously offered against the truth of them, and though they are false, yet it is not false to have remembered them. I perceive that it is one thing to distinguish these things and another to remember that I have often distinguished them when I thought upon them. I remember both that I have often understood these things in the past, and that I am storing up in my memory what I now discern and understand about them, so that later on I can recall what I now understand. Therefore I remember that I have remembered, so that if later on I should call to mind that I was once able to remember these things, it will be by the power of memory that I shall recall it.

FOURTEEN

The same memory contains the feelings of my mind—not in the same way that my mind contains them when it feels them, but in quite a different way, according to a power peculiar to memory. For without rejoicing, I remember that I have rejoiced. Without sorrow, I recollect my past sorrow. And what I once feared, I review without fear; without desire, I call to mind past desire. Sometimes, on the other hand, I remember my past sorrow with joy, and my past joy with sorrow.

This is not to be wondered at as regards the body, for the mind is one thing, the body another. If I therefore remember some past pain of the body with joy, it is not so strange. But this very memory itself is mind—for when we want something remembered, we say, "See that you keep this in mind." And when we forget, we say, "It did not come to my mind," or "It slipped my mind," calling the memory itself the mind.

Since this is so, how is it that, when I remember my past sorrow with joy, the mind has joy while the memory has sorrow? The mind rejoices over the joyfulness that is in it, while the memory is not sad while retaining the sadness in it. Does the memory perchance not belong to the mind? Who will say so? The memory then is, as it were, the belly of the mind, and joy and sadness are like sweet and bitter food. When these are committed to the memory, they are, as it were, passed into the belly, where they may be stowed but not tasted. It is ridiculous to consider this comparison, but yet they are not totally unalike.

But, consider this. It is out of my memory that I say there are four basic emotions of the mind—desire, joy, fear, and sorrow. Whatever I may discuss about them, by dividing each into its own particular kind, and by defining what it is, it is from my memory that I find what to say and bring it out from there. Yet I am not disturbed by these emotions when I call them to mind and remember them. Yes, and before I recalled and brought them back, they were there, and so could be brought forth by recollection. Perhaps as meat is brought up out of the stomach by chewing the cud, these things are brought out of the memory by recollection. Why, then, does the man who is thinking of them not taste in his mouth the sweetness of joy or the bitterness of sorrow? Does the comparison fail in this because it is not alike in all respects? For who would ever willingly speak of it, if every time we named grief or fear we should be compelled to feel sad or fearful? And yet we could not speak of them if we did not find in our memory, not only the sounds of their names according to images impressed on it by our bodily senses, but also the notions of the things themselves, which we never received by any avenue of the flesh. But the mind itself recognized them through the experience of its own passions, committed them to the memory; or else the memory itself retained them without having them actually assigned to it [by the conscious mind].

FIFTEEN

But whether this is done by images or not, who can readily say? Thus, I name a stone, I name the sun, and the things themselves are not present to my senses, but their images are present to my memory. I name a bodily pain, yet it is not present with me when nothing aches. Yet, unless its image was present in my memory, I would not know what to say of it, nor how to tell pain from pleasure. I name bodily health. When I am sound in body, the thing itself is present with me; yet unless its image were also present in my memory, I could not recall what the sound of this name signified. Nor would the sick, when health was named, recognize what was being spoken of, unless the same image were retained by the power of memory, although the thing itself was absent from the body. I name numbers by which we count; and it is not their images but the numbers themselves that are present in my memory. I name the image of the sun, and that image is present in my memory. For I do not recall the image of its image, but the image itself is present to me when I call it to mind. I name *memory*, and I recognize what I name. But where do I recognize it but in the memory itself? Is it also present to itself by its image, and not by itself?

SIXTEEN

When I name *forgetfulness* and recognize what I name, how could I recognize it if I did not remember it? I do not speak of the sound of the name, but the thing which it signifies. If I had forgotten, I could not recognize what that sound meant. When I remember memory, memory itself is, by means of itself, present with itself; but when I remember forgetfulness, there are present both memory and forgetfulness: memory by which I remember, and forgetfulness which I remember.

But what is forgetfulness, but the absence of memory? How then can that be present, so that I remember it, which, when it is present keeps me from remembering? But if we hold in memory what we remember, we could never recognize forgetfulness when we hear it named unless we remembered it. So then, forgetfulness is retained by memory. It is present then, so that we do not forget it. This being the case, are we to suppose that forgetfulness, when we remember it, is present to the memory only through its image rather than by itself? Because if it were present by itself, it would not cause us to remember, but to forget. Who can search this out? Who shall understand how it is?

Lord, I truly toil in this; yes, and in myself. I have become a difficult soil, requiring too much sweat of the brow. For I am not now searching out the regions of the heavens, or measuring the distances of the stars, or inquiring about the weight of the earth. It is I myself who remember, I, the mind. It is not so strange if what I am not should be far from me. But what is nearer to me than myself? And lo, I do not understand the power of my own memory, though I cannot even name myself without it. For what shall I say, when it is clear to me that I remember forgetfulness? Shall I say that what I remember is not in my memory? Or shall I say that forgetfulness is in my memory so that I will not forget? Both of these are most absurd. But what third view is there? How can I say that the image of forgetfulness is retained in my memory, not forgetfulness itself, when I remember it? How could I say this either, seeing that when the image of anything itself is imprinted on the memory, the thing itself must first be present from which the image may be imprinted? For this is the way I remember Carthage, and in this way I remember all the places I have been; this is the way it is with men's faces whom I have seen, and things reported by the other senses. Thus it is with health or sickness of the body. For when these things were present, my memory received images from them, which remain present with me, so that I can look on them and bring them back to mind when I remember them in their absence. If then this forgetfulness is retained in the memory through its image, not through itself, then plainly it was once present itself, so that its image might be taken. But when it was present, how did it write its image in my memory, since forgetfulness by its presence erases even what it finds already recorded? And yet, in whatever way, although it is past conceiving or explaining, I am certain that I remember forgetfulness itself, too, by which is blotted out what we remember.

SEVENTEEN

Great is the power of memory, a fearful thing, O my God, a deep and boundless multiplicity; and this is the mind and this I am myself. What am I then, O my God? What nature am I? A life various and manifold, exceedingly immense. Behold the innumerable plains and caves and caverns of my memory are innumerably full of unnumbered kinds of things—either through images, as in all physical bodies, or by actual presence, as the arts, or by certain notions or impressions, like the emotions of the mind that are retained by the memory even when we no longer feel them, because whatever is in the memory is in the mind. I run over all these, I fly, I dive on this side and on that, as far as I can, and there is no end. The power of memory is as great as the power of life in this mortal life of man.

What shall I do then, O my God, my true life? I will go even beyond this power of mine that is called memory. Yes, I will go beyond it, so that I may approach you, O lovely Light. What do you say to me? See, I am mounting up through my mind toward you who dwell above me. Yes, I now will pass beyond this power of mine that is called memory, desiring to reach you where you may be reached, and to cleave to you where that is possible. For even beasts and birds have memory, otherwise they could not return to their dens and nests, nor do the many other things they do. Nor indeed could they be used in any way except through their memory. I will pass then beyond memory, too, that I may reach him who has separated me from the four-footed beasts and made me wiser than the fowls of the air. So, I will go on beyond memory, but where shall I find you, O truly Good and certain Sweetness? If I find you without my memory, then I cannot retain you in my memory. And how shall I find you, if I do not remember you?

EIGHTEEN

The woman who lost her drachma and searched for it with a light could never have found it unless she had remembered it. And when it was found, how would she know it was the same coin if she did not remember it? I remember having looked for and finding many things, and this I know by it, that when I was searching for any of them, and was asked, "Is this it?" "Is that it?" I said, "No," until the thing I was looking for was offered. But if I had not remembered it—whatever it was—though it had been offered to me, I could not have found it because I failed to recognize it. And so it always is when we look for and find any lost thing. Nevertheless, when anything is lost from sight by chance (not from the memory, as any visible body might be) still its image is retained within us, and we look for it until it is restored to sight; and when it is found, we recognize it by its image within. We do not say that we have found what was lost unless we recognize it, and we cannot recognize it unless we remember it. It was lost to the eye, but it was retained in the memory.

NINETEEN

When the memory itself loses anything, as happens when we forget something and try to recall it, where do we look for it, but in the memory itself? And there, if one thing happens to be offered instead of another, we reject it until we find what we are looking for. And when we find it, we say, "This is it!" We could not say that unless we recognized it, nor recognize it unless we remembered it. Certainly then we had forgotten it. Or, had all of it not been forgotten, and did we look for the part that was missing by the part which we still remembered, as if the memory felt that it could not carry on properly until the missing part was restored to it?

For instance, if we see or think of someone known to us, and having forgotten his name, try to recall it, whatever else occurs does not connect itself with his name, because we are not accustomed to think of that in connection with him. So we go on rejecting these things until something presents itself on which the knowledge we seek rests. And from where does that come, but out of the memory itself? For even when we recognize it as it is brought to mind by someone else, it still comes from memory. For we do not believe it as something new, but upon recollection, agree that what was said was right. But if it had been utterly blotted out of the mind, we would not remember it even when reminded of it. For we have not as yet utterly forgotten what we remember as having forgotten. What we have lost and utterly forgotten, we cannot even search for.

TWENTY

How do I seek you, then, O Lord? For when I seek you, my God, I seek a happy life. I will seek you that my soul may live. For my body lives by my soul, and my soul lives by you. How then do I seek a happy life, seeing that I do not have it until I can rightly say, "It is enough!" How do I seek it? By remembering, as though I had forgotten it, remembering that I had forgotten it? Or by desiring to learn it as something unknown, either never having known, or having so forgotten as not even to remember that it had been forgotten? Is not a happy life what all seek, and is there anyone who does not desire it? Where have they known it, so that they desire it? Where have they seen it, that they love it so much? Somehow we have it, but how I do not know.

There is indeed a way in which one has it and then is happy, and there are some who are happy in the hope of having it. These have it in a lesser way than those who have it in very fact; yet they are better off than those who are neither happy in fact nor in hope. Yet even these, if they did not have it in some way, would not so greatly desire to be happy—and that they do desire it is most certain. How they have known it then, I do not know. By what sort of knowledge they have it, I do not know, and I am perplexed whether it is in the memory—for in that case, we would have been happy once.

I do not now inquire as to whether everyone was happy separately, or happy in that man who first sinned, in whom also we all died, and from whom we are all born with misery. I only ask whether the happy life is in the memory. For we could not love it if we did not know it. We hear the name, and we all confess that we desire the thing, for we are not delighted with the mere sound. When a Greek hears it in Latin, he is not delighted, not knowing what is being spoken. But we Latins are delighted, as he would be too, if he heard it in Greek; because the thing itself that Greeks and Latins and men of all other tongues long for so earnestly is neither Greek nor Latin. It is therefore known to all, for could they with one voice be asked, "Do you want to be happy?" they would answer, without doubt, "We do." And this could not be unless happiness itself, signified by the name, were retained in their memory.

TWENTY-ONE

But is it the same as when one who has seen Carthage remembers it? No. For a happy life is not seen with the eye, because it is not a body. Is it the same as when we remember numbers? No. For the one who has these in his knowledge does not have to look further to reach them. But a happy life we have in our knowledge and therefore love it, and yet we still desire to attain it, so that we may be happy. Is it the same as when we remember eloquence, then? No. Upon hearing this name, some who are not yet eloquent and desire to be so call eloquence to mind. Through their bodily senses they have observed others to be eloquent, and were delighted by it and wanted to be like them, though actually they would not have been delighted without some inward knowledge of eloquence, nor want to be like them unless they were delighted by it. But in the case of the happy life, we do not experience it in others through any bodily sense.

Do we remember happiness then in the same way we remember joy? Possibly. For I remember my joy even when I am sad, as I remember a happy life even when I am unhappy. Nor did I ever see, hear, smell, taste, or touch my joy with my bodily senses, but I experienced it in my mind when I rejoiced, and the knowledge of it stuck in my memory, so that I can recall it—at times with disgust, at other times with longing, according to the nature of the things that I remember having enjoyed. For I have been immersed in a sort of joy even from foul things that I now abhor and utterly detest when I recall them. At other times

I rejoiced in good and honest things that I recall with longing, although they may no longer be present. In that case I recall former joy with sorrow.

Where then, and when, did I experience my happy life that I should remember and love and long for it? Mine is not an isolated case, nor is it that of some few besides me, but all of us desire to be happy. Unless by some certain knowledge we knew what a happy life is, we could not desire it with such certainty. But how is this, that if two men are asked whether they would go to the wars, one might answer that he would and the other that he would not? But if they were asked whether they wanted to be happy, they would instantly, without any hesitation, say they would; and for no other reason would the one choose to go to the wars and the other not, but to be happy. Is it possible that as one looks for his joy in one thing, another in another, all agree in their desire to be happy? In the same way, if they were asked, they would agree that they wished to have joy, and would they call this joy a happy life? Then, although one obtains joy by one means, another by another, both have the same goal they try to reach— joy. Since joy is a thing which all must say they have experienced, it is therefore found in the memory and recognized whenever the name of a happy life is mentioned.

TWENTY-TWO

Far be it, Lord, far be it from the heart of your servant who is confessing here to you, far be it from me to think that I am happy, be the joy what it may. For there is a joy that is not given to the ungodly, but to those who love you for your own sake, whose joy is you yourself. And this is the happy life: to rejoice in you, of you, for you. This is true joy and there is no other. They who think there is another seek some other, and not the true joy. Yet their will is not turned except by some semblance of joy.

TWENTY-THREE

Is it, then, not certain that all wish to be happy, inasmuch as those who do not wish to joy in you (which is the only happy life) do not truly desire the happy life? Or do all men desire this, but *the flesh strives against the Spirit and the Spirit against the flesh*, so that they cannot do what they wish to do? Do they then settle on that which they can do, and are content with that, because they do not desire strongly enough what they cannot do to make them able to do it? For if I ask anyone if he would rather rejoice in truth or in falsehood, he will hesitate as little to say, "In the truth," as he would to say that he desires to be happy. But a happy life is joy in the truth, for this is rejoicing in you, who are the Truth, O God, my Light, *the Health of my countenance and my God*. This happy life all desire; all desire this life that is the only happy life, for all desire to rejoice in the truth. I have met with many who would deceive others; none who want to be deceived. And when they love a happy life, which is nothing else than rejoicing in the truth, then they also love the truth—which they could not love if there were not some knowledge of it in their memory. Why then do they not rejoice in it? Why are they not happy? Because they are more strongly occupied with other things that have more power to make them miserable than that which they so dimly remember has to make them happy. For there is yet a little light in men; let them walk, let them walk, *lest the darkness overtake them*.

But why does truth generate hatred, and why does your servant, preaching the truth, become their enemy, since a happy life is loved, which is nothing else but rejoicing in the truth?

How is this so unless the truth is loved in such a way that those who love something else want what they love to be the truth? And because they do not want to be deceived, they do not want to be convinced that they are. Therefore they hate the truth, for the sake of the thing they love instead of the truth.

They love the truth when it enlightens, they hate it when it reproves. Since they would not be deceived, yet would deceive, they love it when it reveals itself to them, but hate it when it reveals them to themselves. Thus the truth shall repay them, by exposing those who do not wish to be exposed by it, and yet not revealing itself to them. Thus, thus, yes, thus does the mind of man—blind, sick, foul, and ill-behaved—wish to be hidden, but does not want anything hidden from it. But the very opposite happens. The mind is not hidden from the truth, while the truth remains hidden from it. Happy then will it be, when without any other distraction, it shall rejoice in that sole Truth by which all things are true.

TWENTY-FOUR

See what a space I have covered in my memory in seeking you, O Lord! And I have not found you outside it, nor have I found anything concerning you but what I retained in my memory ever since I learned of you. Since I learned of you I have not forgotten you. Where I found truth, there I found my God, the Truth itself. And since I learned this I have not forgotten it. Thus since the time I learned of you, you have resided in my memory. There I find you when I call you to remembrance, and delight in you. These are my holy delights that you have given me in your mercy, being mindful of my poverty.

TWENTY-FIVE

But where do you abide in my memory, O Lord? Where do you abide there? What kind of dwelling place have you made for yourself there? What kind of sanctuary have you built there for yourself? You have given this honor to my memory, to abide in it; but in what part of it you dwell—that I am pondering. For in thinking about you, I passed beyond such parts of it as the animals have, for I did not find you there among corporeal things. And I came to those areas in which I stored the affections of my mind, and did not find you there. Then I entered into the innermost seat of my mind—which the mind has in my memory, since the mind remembers itself—but you were not there. For as you are not a corporeal image, nor the affection of a living being (as when we rejoice, sympathize with, desire, fear, remember, forget, or the like), so neither are you the mind itself. Because you are the Lord God of the mind, and all these things change, but you remain unchangeable over them all—and yet you have granted to dwell in my memory ever since I learned of you. So why do I now seek to know the part of my memory in which you dwell, as if there were places in the mind? Assuredly, you dwell in it since I have remembered you ever since I learned of you, and since I find you there when I call you to remembrance.

TWENTY-SIX

Where then did I find you that I might learn of you? You were not in my memory before I learned of you. Where did I find you, that I might learn of you, but in yourself, above myself. Place there is none; we go backward and forward, and there is no "place" [location]. Everywhere, O Truth, you hear those who ask counsel of you, and answer all of them at once, though they ask your counsel on many different things. You answer them clearly, though they do not all hear clearly. All consult you on whatever they wish, though they do not always hear back what they wish. He is your best servant who looks not so much to hear what he desires from you, as to desire that which he hears from you.

TWENTY-SEVEN

Too late have I loved you, O Beauty, ancient yet ever new. Too late have I loved you! And behold, you were within, but I was outside, searching for you there—plunging, deformed amid those fair forms that you had made. You were with me, but I was not with you. Things held me far from you, which, unless they were in you, did not exist at all. You called and shouted, and burst my deafness. You gleamed and shone upon me, and chased away my blindness. You breathed fragrant odors on me, and I held back my breath, but now I pant for you. I tasted, and now I hunger and thirst for you. You touched me, and now I yearn for your peace.

TWENTY-EIGHT

When I come to be united with you with my whole self, I shall have no more sorrow or labor, and my life shall be wholly alive, being wholly full of you! You lift up the one you fill, but I am still a burden to myself, because I am not full of you. Lamentable joys strive with joyous sorrows: and on which side the victory will be I do not know. Woe is me! Lord, have mercy on me. My evil sorrows strive with my good joys; and I do not know on which side the victory may be. Woe is me! Lord, have mercy on me! Woe is me! See! I do not hide my wounds; you are the Physician, I the sick. You are the merciful,

I the miserable one. Is not the life of man upon earth all trial? Who wishes for troubles and difficulties? You command them to be endured, not to be loved. No man loves what he endures, though he may love to endure. For though he rejoices that he endures, he would rather there were nothing for him to endure. In adversity, I long for prosperity; in prosperity I fear adversity. What middle ground is there between these two—where the life of man is not all trial? Woe to the prosperities of the world, twice woe—woe from fear of adversity and woe from corruption of joy! Woe to the adversities of this world, twice woe, and triple woe: woe from longing for prosperity, woe because adversity itself is a hard thing, and woe for fear that it may make a shipwreck of our endurance! Is not the life of man upon earth all trial without intermission?

TWENTY-NINE

And all my hope is only in your exceeding great mercy. Give what you command, and command what you will. You command self-restraint, and "When I knew," said one, "that no man can be continent unless God gave it, that was a point of wisdom also to know whose gift it is." For by self-restraint, truly, we are bound up and brought back together into wholeness, whereas we had been splintered in many ways. For he loves you too little who loves anything else with you that he does not love for you. O Love, who ever burns and is never quenched! O Charity, my God! Enkindle me. You command continence; give me what you command and command what you will.

THIRTY

Truly you command that I should be continent from the lust of *the flesh, the lust of the eyes, and the pride of life*. You have commanded self-restraint from fornication, and as for wedlock itself, you have counseled something better than what you have permitted. And since you gave it, it was done, even before I became a minister of your Sacrament. But there yet lives in my memory (of which I have spoken at length) the images of such things as my bad habits had fixed there. These rush into my thoughts when I am awake, but in my sleep they not only seem pleasurable, but even to obtain my consent in what very closely resembles reality. Yes, the illusion of the image so far prevails in my soul and in my flesh, that when I am asleep, false visions persuade me to what the true ones cannot when I am awake. Am I not myself at such times, O Lord my God? There is yet so much difference between myself and myself in that instant in which I pass from waking to sleeping, or return from sleeping to waking! Where is reason, then, which resists such suggestions when awake and remains unmoved when such suggestions are urged on it? Is it closed up when my eyes are closed? Is it lulled asleep with the senses of the body? But from where is it that often, even in sleep, we resist and, mindful of our purpose and continuing most chastely in it, give no assent to such enticements? And there is yet so much difference that, when it happens otherwise, upon waking we return to peace of conscience, and by this very difference in the two states, discover that it was not we who did it, while we feel sorry that in some way it was done in us.

Is not your hand able, O Almighty God, to heal all the diseases of my soul and by your more abundant grace able to quench even the lascivious motions of my sleep? You will increase your gifts in me more and more, Lord, that my soul may follow me to you, disengaged from the bird-lime of lust; that it may not be in rebellion against itself, and may not commit in dreams through these sensual images those debasing corruptions, even to pollution of the flesh, nor give consent to them. For it is not too hard for the Almighty to work this—that nothing of this sort should have the very least influence over the pure affections of a sleeper, not even so slight a one as a thought might hold back—not just sometime during this life, but even at my present age, for you are *able to do more than we can ask or think*. But what I still am in this kind of evil, I have confessed to my good Lord, rejoicing with trembling in that which you have given me, and bemoaning that in which I am still imperfect; trusting that you will perfect your mercies in me, even to fullness of peace, which my outward and inward man shall have with you, when *death is swallowed up in victory*.

THIRTY-ONE

There is another *evil of the day*, which I wish were *sufficient unto it*. For by eating and drinking we repair the daily decays of the body, until you *destroy both food and belly*, when you shall slay my emptiness with a wonderful fullness, and clothe this corruptible with an eternal incorruption. But for the present, necessity is sweet to me, and I fight against this sweetness lest I be taken captive by it. I carry on a daily war by fastings, often bringing my body into subjection. And my pains are expelled by pleasure. For hunger and thirst are, in a manner, pains. They burn and kill like a fever unless the medicine of nourishment comes to relieve us. Since they are readily at hand from the comfort we receive through your gifts (with which land, water and air serve our weakness), our calamity is called pleasure.

This much you have taught me, that I should train myself to take food as medicine. But while I am passing from the discomfort of emptiness to the satisfaction of fullness, in that very passage the snare of lust lies in wait for me. For that passage itself is pleasurable; there is no other way to pass to that state of fullness, and necessity forces us to pass. And although health is the reason for eating and drinking, yet a dangerous delight accompanies it, and frequently tries to control it in order that I may do for enjoyment's sake what I say I do, or wish to do, for health's sake. Health and pleasure do not have the same limits. What is enough for health is too little for pleasure. And it is often questionable whether it is the necessary care of the body which still asks nourishment, or whether a sensual snare of desire wants to be served. In this uncertainty, my unhappy soul rejoices and prepares in it an excuse to shield itself, glad that it is not clearly apparent what would suffice for the moderation of health, so that under the cloak of health it may conceal the business of pleasure. These temptations I try to resist daily, and I call your right hand to my aid, and refer my perplexities to you, because as yet I have no clear resolution in this matter.

I hear the voice of my God commanding, *Let not your heart be overcharged with immoderate indulgence and drunkenness.* Drunkenness is far from me; you will have mercy that it may never come near me. But overeating sometimes creeps up on your servant; you will have mercy that it may depart from me. For no man can be continent unless you give it. You give us many things that we pray for, and whatever good we have received before we prayed, we received it from you. Yes, we received it from you that we might afterward know that we received it from you. I was never a drunkard, but I have known drunkards who were made sober by you. It was from you, then, that they who never were drunkards might not be so, and it was your gift that both might know that it was from you.

I heard another voice of yours: "Do not follow your lusts and refrain yourself from your pleasures." And by your grace I have heard that which I have greatly loved: *Neither if we eat are we the better; nor if we do not eat are we the worse.* Which is to say, neither shall the one make me abound, nor the other make me miserable. I heard another also: *For I have learned in whatever state I am, therewith to be content; I know how to abound and how to suffer need. I can do all things through Christ who strengthens me.* See there a soldier of the heavenly camp—the dust as we are. But remember, Lord, *that we are dust,* and that of dust you have made man, and *he was lost and is found.* He [Paul] could not do this by his own strength, because he whom I so love who said these things through the breath of your inspiration, was made of the same dust. He says, *I can do all things through him who strengthens me.* Strengthen me, that I may be able; grant what you command, and command what you will. He confesses to have received, and when he glories, he glories in the Lord. Another person I have heard begging that he might receive: "Take from me," he says, "the greediness of the belly." From this it appears to me, O my holy God, that when that is done which you command, it is by your gift that it is done.

You have taught me, good Father, that *to the pure all things are pure*; but that it is *evil to the man who gives offense in eating.* And that *every creature of yours is good,* and *nothing is to be refused that is received with thanksgiving*; and that *food does not commend us to God,* and that *no man should judge us in food or drink*; that he *who eats should not despise him who does not eat*; and that he *who does not eat should not judge him who eats.* These things have I learned, thanks and praise be to you, my God, my Master, knocking at the door of my ears, enlightening my heart, delivering me out of all temptation. I do not fear the uncleanness of food, but the uncleanness of lust. I know that Noah was permitted to eat all kinds of flesh that was good for food. I know also that Elijah was fed with flesh; that John, endued with a wonderful abstinence, was not polluted by eating locusts alive, which he fed on. I know, too, that Esau was deceived by craving lentils, and that David blamed himself for desiring a drink of water; and that our King was tempted, not by flesh, but bread. Therefore the people in the wilderness deserved to be reproved, too—not so much for desiring flesh, but because, in their desire for food, they murmured against the Lord.

Placed, then, amid these temptations, I strive daily against lust for food and drink. For it is not the kind [of temptation] that I can resolve to cut off once and for all, and never touch it afterward, as I did with fornication. The bridle of the throat, therefore, is to be held moderately between slackness and strictness. And who is he, O Lord, who is not carried in some degree beyond the bounds of necessity in it? Whoever he is, he is a great one! Let him magnify your name. But I am not such a one, for *I am a sinful man*. Yet I, too, magnify your name, and he who has *overcome the world* makes intercession to you for my sins, numbering me among the weak members of his body, because *your eyes have looked on my imperfect being and in your book shall all be written*.

THIRTY-TWO

I am not greatly concerned with all the attractions of sweet scents. When they are absent, I do not miss them; when they are present, I do not refuse them, yet am ready to be without them. So I seem to myself, though possibly I am deceived. For that is also a lamentable darkness that conceals my capabilities from me, so that my mind, inquiring into itself concerning its own powers, does not readily dare to believe itself, because even what is already in it is largely concealed unless it is exposed by experience. And no one ought to be secure in this life, the whole of which is called a temptation, so that he who has been made better from worse may also from better be made worse. Our only hope, our only confidence, our only assured promise, is your mercy.

THIRTY-THREE

The delights of the ear had more firmly entangled and conquered me, but you have unbound and liberated me. Now, I still find some repose in those melodies into which your words breathe soul, when they are sung with a sweet and trained voice. Yet I do not allow myself to be held by them, for I can disengage myself from them when I wish. But with the words which are the life of such melodies and by which they gain admission into me, they seek a place of some honor in my heart, and I can scarcely assign them a fitting one. For at times I seem to myself to give them more honor than is proper, sensing that our minds are more devoutly and fervently inflamed in devotion by the holy words themselves when they are sung this way, than when they are not. I notice that the different emotions of my spirit, by their sweet variety, have their appropriate expressions in the voice and singing, by some hidden relationship that stirs them up. But this gratification of my flesh, which must not be allowed to take control over my mind, often beguiles me. My feelings do not serve reason, so as to follow it patiently, but after having gained admission for the sake of reason, strive to grab the reins and take the lead. Thus in these things I sin without knowing it, but realize it afterward.

At other times, anxiously shunning this very deception, I err by being too strict, and sometimes to the degree of wishing to have every melody of sweet music to which David's Psalter is often sung banished both from my ears and from the Church itself. That way seems safer which I remember having often heard was followed by Athanasius, bishop of Alexandria. He made the reader of the psalm utter it with such a slight inflection of the voice that it was more like speaking than singing. Yet, again, when I remember the tears I shed at the songs of your Church in the early days of my recovered faith, and how even now I am moved not by the singing, but by what is being sung, when they are sung with a clear voice and skillful modulation, I recognize once more the great usefulness of this practice. Thus I vacillate between the perilous pleasure and proved soundness—inclined rather to approve the custom of singing in the church (though not pronouncing it as an irrevocable opinion), so that the weaker minds may rise to the feeling of devotion by the delight of the ears. Yet when I happen to be more moved by the singing than by what is being sung, I confess that I have sinned gravely, and then would rather not have heard the singing. See my condition now! Weep with me and weep for me, you who can so control your inward feelings that good results follow. For you who do not act this way, these things do not concern you. But O my God, hear me and look upon me, and have mercy on me and heal me, you in whose presence I have become a puzzle to myself; and *this is my infirmity*.

THIRTY-FOUR

There remain the delights of these eyes of my flesh, about which to make my confession in the hearing of the ears of your temple, those brotherly and devout ears, and so to conclude the temptations of *the lust of the flesh* that still assault me, as I groan earnestly, *desiring to be clothed upon with my house from heaven*.

My eyes love beautiful and varied forms, and bright and soft colors. Let these not occupy my soul; let God rather possess it, who made these things *very good* indeed—for he is my Good, not these. Yes, these affect me during the whole waking day. No rest is given me from them, as there sometimes is in silence from music and from all voices. For that queen of colors, the light, flooding all we look upon, wherever I am during the day, gliding past me in various forms, soothes me when I am busied about other things and not noticing it. And it entwines itself so strongly, that, if it is suddenly withdrawn, I look longingly for it, and if it is long absent, my mind is saddened.

O Light that Tobias saw when, with his eyes closed in blindness, he taught his son the way of life, and led the way himself with the feet of charity, never going astray. Or that Light which Isaac saw when, his bodily eyes so dim by reason of old age that he could not see, it was granted him to bless his sons without knowing which was which, but in blessing them to know them. Or which Jacob saw, blind through great age but with an illumined heart, when he shed light upon the different races of people yet to come—foreshown in the persons of his sons—and he laid his hands, mystically crossed, on his grandchildren, the sons of Joseph, not as their father by his outward eye corrected them, but as he himself inwardly discerned them. This is the true Light, the only one, and all who see and love it are one. But that corporeal light of which I spoke seasons the life of this world for those who blindly love it with an enticing and fatal sweetness. They who know how to praise you for this earthly light, "O God, Creator of All," and sing of it in your hymns, but are not taken up with it in their sleep. Such I desire to be. I resist these seductions of the eyes, lest my feet by which I walk on your path be entangled. And I lift up my inward eyes to you, that you would be pleased to *pluck my feet out of the snare*. You do repeatedly pluck them out, for they are entangled. You do not cease to pluck them out, but I constantly remain fast in the snares set round me on all sides. For you *shall neither slumber nor sleep, who keep Israel.*

What innumerable things, made by various arts and products, in our clothing, shoes, vessels and every kind of work, in pictures, too, and various images—and these far in excess of all necessary and moderate use, and all devotional significance, men have added for the enthrallment of their own eyes! Outwardly they follow what they make themselves, and inwardly forsake him by whom they themselves were made—yes, and destroying that which he made in them!

I also sing a hymn to you, my God and my Joy, for these things, and offer a sacrifice of praise to my Sanctifier for all those beautiful designs that pass through men's minds and are conveyed to artistic hands, coming from that Beauty which is above our souls, which my soul sighs after day and night. But as for the makers and followers of those outward beauties, they derive from that Beauty their power of judging them, but not of using them. And this power, too, is there, though they do not see it, so they might not wander, but keep their strength for you and not dissipate it on delicious lassitudes. And though I speak this way and see this, I, too, get my steps entangled with these outward beauties, but you rescue me. O Lord, you rescue me, *because your lovingkindness is ever before my eyes.* For I am caught miserably, but you rescue me mercifully. Sometimes I am not even aware of this, not having become wholly entangled. At other times, the rescue is painful, because I was held fast in them.

THIRTY-FIVE

To this is added another form of temptation, more complex in its peril. For besides the *lust of the flesh*, which lies in the gratification of all our senses and pleasures, whose slaves wander far from you, are wasted and perish, the soul has, through those same bodily senses, a certain vain and curious desire, cloaked under the name of knowledge and learning—not delighting in the flesh, but in making experiments through the flesh. This longing, since it originates in an appetite for knowledge, and since sight is the sense mainly used to acquire knowledge, is called in divine language *the lust of the eyes*. For seeing properly belongs to the eye, yet we use this word in connection with the other senses, too, when we exercise them in the search for knowledge. For we do not say, "Listen how it glows!" or "Smell how it glistens," or "Taste how it shines," or "Feel how it gleams," for all these are said to be seen. Yet we not only say, "See how it shines," which the eyes alone can perceive; but we also say, "See how it sounds, see how it smells, see how it tastes, and see how hard it is." And so the general experience of the senses, as we said, is called *the lust of the eyes*, because the office of seeing, though properly belonging to the eyes, is applied to the other senses by analogy when they seek after any knowledge.

By this it may be more clearly discerned when the object of the senses is pleasure and when it is curiosity. For pleasure seeks objects that are beautiful, melodious, fragrant, tasty, soft; but curiosity, for the sake of novelty, seeks the very opposite as well, not in order to experience their trouble, but from the passion of experimenting and knowing.

What pleasure is there to see in a mangled corpse that which makes you shudder? And yet, if it is lying near, we flock to it, to be made sad and to turn pale. They fear they will see it in their sleep, as if anyone had forced them to look at it when they were awake, or any report of its beauty had attracted them to it! Thus it is also with the other senses, which would take too long to go through. From this malady of curiosity come all those strange sights exhibited in the theater. From it men go on to search out the secret powers of nature (which do not pertain to us) which to know brings no profit, and which men desire to know simply for the sake of knowing. From this malady, too, with the same goal of gaining perverted knowledge, we consult the magical arts. Even in religion itself God is tempted when signs and wonders are demanded of him—not desired for any saving purpose, but merely to make trial of him.

In such a vast wilderness as this, full of snares and dangers, I have cut many of them off and thrust them out of my heart, as you have given me power to do, O God of my salvation. Yet when do I dare say—since so many things of this kind buzz on all sides about our daily life—when do I dare say that nothing of this sort engages my attention or causes an idle interest in me? True, the theaters no longer carry me away nowadays, nor do I care to know the courses of the stars, nor did my soul ever consult departed spirits. I detest all unhallowed rites. But yet, O Lord my God, to whom I owe humble and single-hearted service, by what subtlety of suggestion does the enemy tempt me to require some sign from you! But I beseech you by our King, and by our pure and holy country Jerusalem, that as any consent on my part to such thoughts is far from me, so may it ever be farther and farther. But when I pray to you for the salvation of anyone, my goal and intention is far different. For you do what you will, and you give me the grace and will give me the grace to follow you willingly.

Nevertheless, in how many petty and contemptible things is our curiosity tempted daily, and who can recount how often we give in to it? How often, when people are telling idle tales, do we begin, as if we were tolerating them to keep from offending the weak, and then gradually begin to take an interest in them! I do not go nowadays to the circus to see a dog chasing a hare, but if by chance I pass such a chase in the field, it may distract me even from some serious thought, and draw me after it—not that I turn aside the body of my horse, but by the inclination of my mind. And unless you, reminding me of my weakness, speedily warn me to lift my thoughts to you above the sight, or to despise it wholly and pass on by, I, vain creature that I am, will stand gazing at it.

When sitting at home, my attention is often distracted by a lizard catching flies, or by a spider entangling flies as they rush into her web. Is the feeling of curiosity different because they are but small creatures? I go on from such distractions to praise you, the wonderful Creator and Disposer of all things; but that is not what first attracts my attention. It is one thing to get up quickly; it is another not to fall. And of such things my life is full, and my only hope is your wonderful, great mercy. For when this heart of ours becomes the receptacle of such things, and bears multitudes of these abounding vanities, then our prayers are often interrupted and disturbed by them, and while in your presence we direct the voice of our heart to your ears, such a great concern as this is interrupted by the influx of I know not what idle thoughts.

THIRTY-SIX

Shall we, then, reckon curiosity among the things to be condemned? Or shall anything restore us to hope but your complete mercy, since you have begun to change us? And you know to what extent you have already changed me, first healing me of the lust of vindicating myself, so that you might forgive all the rest of my *iniquities* and heal all my *infirmities*, and *redeem* my life from corruption, and *crown me with tender mercies and loving-kindness*, and *satisfy* my desire *with good things*; you curbed my pride with fear and tamed my neck to your yoke. And now I bear it and it is *light* to me, because you have so promised and have so made it. And in very truth it was, but I knew it not when I feared to take it up.

But, O Lord, you alone reign without pride, because you are the only true Lord and have no lord. Tell me, has this third kind of temptation left me, or can it ever leave me throughout this lifetime—the desire to be feared and loved by men for no other purpose but that I may enjoy that which is no joy? It is a miserable life and an unseemly ostentation! From this especially it comes that we do not love you nor have a holy fear of you. And therefore you *resist the proud and give grace to the humble.* Yes, you thunder down on the ambitious designs of the world, *and the foundations of the hills tremble.*

Because certain offices of human society make it necessary for the holder to be loved and feared of men, the adversary of our true blessedness presses hard on us, spreading everywhere his snares of "Well done, well done." Greedily reaching for them, we may be caught unawares and separate our joy from your truth and fix it in the deceits of men, and take pleasure in being loved and feared—not for your sake, but in your stead. Having been made like our adversary, then, he may have us for his own, not in the harmony of charity but in the fellowship of punishment. He aspired to *exalt his throne in the north*, so that we men, dark and cold, might serve him who would become a perverse and distorted imitation of you.

But we, O Lord, lo, we are your *little flock*. Possess us as yours. Stretch your wings over us, and let us take refuge under them.

Be our glory. Let us be loved for your sake and let your Word be reverenced in us. Those who desire to be praised by the men you condemn will not be defended by men when you judge, nor delivered when you pass sentence. But when—not as when the sinner is praised in the desires of his soul, nor when the unrighteous is blessed in his ungodliness—but when a man is praised for some gift which you have given him, and he is more gratified by the praise for himself than that he possesses the gift for which he is praised, such a one also is praised while you blame. Truly, the man who praised him is better than the one being praised. For the one took pleasure in the gift of God in man, while the other was better pleased with the gift of man than that of God.

THIRTY-SEVEN

We are assaulted by these temptations daily, O Lord; without ceasing we are tried. Our daily furnace is the human tongue. And in this respect, too, you command continence [self-mastery] of us. Give what you command and command what you will. You know the groanings of my heart on this matter, and the rivers that flood my eyes. For I cannot ascertain how far I am clean of this plague, and I stand in great fear of my secret faults which your eyes perceive but mine do not. For in other kinds of temptation I have some way of examining myself; in this, hardly any. For in keeping my mind from the pleasures of the flesh and from idle curiosity, I see how much I have been able to do without them, either voluntarily foregoing them or not having them available. Then I ask myself how much more or less troublesome it is to me not to have them. Riches may be desired that they may serve some one of these lusts, or two, or all three of them. If the soul cannot tell whether it despises riches when it has them, it may cast them aside so that it may prove itself in this way. But to be without praise and to test our abilities in that regard, must we live wickedly, or lead a life so abandoned and atrocious that no one could know us without detesting us? What greater madness could be said or thought? But if praise is usual, and if it ought to accompany a good life and good works, we ought to forego its company as little as we would the good life itself. Yet I cannot tell whether I shall be contented or troubled by being without something unless I am deprived of it.

What, then, do I confess to you, O Lord, in this kind of temptation? What, but that I am delighted with praise, but with truth itself more than with praise? For if it were proposed to me, whether I would rather, being mad or in error on all things, be praised by all men, or being consistent and well assured in the truth, be blamed by all, I see which I would choose. Yet I would rather that the approval of another should not even increase my joy for any good in me. I admit, though, that it does increase it, and more than that, that criticism diminishes it.

When I am troubled at this misery of mine, an excuse presents itself to me—of what value it is, only you know, O God, for it leaves me uncertain. Here it is: It is not self-control [continency] alone that you have commanded of us (that is, that we should hold back our love from certain things), but also righteousness as well (that is, upon what to bestow our love), and have wished us to love not only you but also our neighbor. Often when I am gratified by intelligent praise, I appear to myself to be pleased by the competence or insight I see in my neighbor. In the same way, I seem to be sorry for the defect in him when I hear him criticize either what he does not understand or what is good. For I am sometimes grieved at the praise I get, either when those things are praised in me that I dislike in myself, or when lesser or trifling goods are more valued than they ought to be. But again, how do I know whether I am affected like this because I do not want him who praises me to differ from me about myself—not being influenced by consideration for him, but because those same good things that please me in myself please me more when they please someone else as well? For, in a sense, I am not praised when my judgment of myself is not praised, whenever either those things that displease me are praised, or those that please me less are praised more. It seems then that I am uncertain about myself in this matter.

Behold, O Truth, in you I see that I ought not to be moved at my own praises for my own sake, but for the good of my neighbor. And whether this is so with me, I do not know. For concerning this I know less of myself than you do. I beseech you now, O my God, reveal me to myself, too, that I may confess to my brethren who are to pray for me where I find myself weak. Once again, let me examine myself more diligently. If, in the praise I receive I am moved with consideration for the good of my neighbor, why am I less moved if someone else is unjustly criticized than if it be myself? Why am I more irritated by reproach cast upon me than at that cast upon another in my presence with the same injustice? Do I not know this also? Or is it finally that I deceive myself, and do not the truth before you in my heart and speech? Put such madness far from me, O Lord, lest my own mouth be to me *the sinner's oil to anoint my head*.

THIRTY-EIGHT

I am poor and needy; yet I am better when in secret groanings I am displeased with myself and seek your mercy until what is lacking in my defective condition is renewed and made complete in that peace which the eye of the proud does not know.

The word that comes out of the mouth, and the actions known to men, bring with them a most dangerous temptation from the love of praise, which, to establish a certain glory of our own solicits and collects men's compliments. It tempts, even when I reprove myself for it within myself, on the very ground that it is reproved. Often a man glories even more vainly in his very scorn of praise. And so he is no longer avoiding vainglory when he glories in his scorn of vainglory.

THIRTY-NINE

Within us, also, is another evil, arising out of the same kind of temptation, by which men become vain, pleasing themselves in themselves, though they do not please nor displease nor aim at pleasing others. But by pleasing themselves they greatly displease you. They do not merely take pleasure in things that are not good as if they were good, but take pleasure in your good things as if they were their own; or if, acknowledging the good things to be yours, they think they deserve them, or even if they regard them as from your grace, they do not use them with brotherly rejoicing, but begrudge that same grace to others. In all these and similar perils and labors, you see the trembling of my heart. It is not so much that I never inflict these wounds on myself, as that they are ever anew healed by you.

FORTY

Where have you not walked with me, O Truth, teaching me what to avoid and what to desire when I submitted to you what I could see here below and asked your counsel? With my external senses I surveyed the world as I was able, and observed the life that my body derives from me and from these senses themselves. From this I advanced inwardly into the recesses of memory—those various and spacious chambers, wonderfully filled with unnumbered wealth. I considered and was afraid, and could discern none of these things without you, and found none of them to be you. It was not I, myself, who discovered these things, I, who went over them all and labored to distinguish and evaluate everything according to its worth, taking some things from the report of my senses, asking questions about others that I felt to be mixed up with myself, numbering and distinguishing the reporters themselves. Then, in the vast storehouse of my memory I examined some things carefully, relegating others to the background, taking out others into the light. Yet it was not myself who did these things—that is, the power by which I did them was not my own. Nor was it you, for you are the unfailing light that I consulted concerning all these things, as to whether they were, what they were, and what their real value was. And I heard you teaching and commanding me. And this I often do. It delights me, as far as I can be freed from necessary duties, to have recourse to this pleasure.

But in all these that I go over in consultation with you, I can find no safe place for my soul but in you, in whom all my scattered members may be gathered, so that nothing about me may depart from you. And sometimes you introduce me to a most rare affection in my inmost soul, an inexplicable sweetness that seems to have nothing in it that would not belong to the life to come if it were perfected in me. But by these wretched weights of mine, I relapse again into these lower things, am swept back by my old customs, and am held. I weep greatly, yet I am greatly held. To such an extent does the burden of bad habits weigh us down. I can stay in this condition, but I would not; I would stay there, but I cannot; in both ways, I am miserable.

FORTY-ONE

And thus I have reflected on the weariness of my sins in that threefold lust, and have called your right hand to my help. For with a wounded heart I have seen your brightness, and being beaten back, I said, "Who can attain to it? *I am cut off from before your eyes!*" You are the Truth who presides over all things, but I, through my covetousness, would not indeed forego you, but wished to possess a lie along with you, as no one wishes to speak so falsely as to be ignorant of the truth itself. So then, I lost you, because you do not stoop to be enjoyed along with a lie.

FORTY-TWO

Whom could I find to reconcile me to you? Was I to solicit angels? By what prayers? By what sacraments? Many seeking to return to you, and not able of themselves, have, as I hear, tried this, have fallen into a desire for curious visions, and have been deemed worthy to be deluded. For they, being exalted, sought you by the pride of learning, thrusting themselves forward instead of beating their breasts. And so, by a correspondence of heart, they drew to themselves the princes of the air, as conspirators and allies of their pride, by whom through the power of magic they were deceived—seeking a mediator by whom they might be cleansed and *there was none*. For it was the devil himself, *transforming himself into an angel of light*. And he allured proud flesh all the more in that he was without a fleshly body. For they were mortal and sinful; but you, Lord, to whom they proudly sought to be reconciled, are immortal and sinless. But a mediator between God and man must have something in him like God, something in him like men, lest being only like man, he should be far from God, and being only like God, should be too unlike man and so not a mediator. In your secret judgment, then, pride deserved to be deluded by that deceitful mediator who has one thing in common with man: that is sin. Another he would appear to have in common with God: not being clothed with the mortality of flesh, and so would boast himself to be immortal. But since the *wages of sin is death*, this he has in common with mankind, that with them he is condemned to death.

FORTY-THREE

But the true Mediator, whom you have pointed out to the humble in your secret mercy, and sent, that by his example they too might learn that same humility—that *Mediator between God and man, the Man Christ Jesus*, appeared between mortal sinners and the immortal Just One—mortal, as men are mortal; just, as God is just; so that because the wages of righteousness is life and peace, he might cancel the death of justified sinners by a righteousness united with God. He was willing to undergo death in common with them. Hence he was shown forth to holy men of old, so that they, through faith in his Passion to come, even as we through faith in it as already past, might be saved. For as Man, he was Mediator; but as the Word, he was not in the middle between God and man, because he was equal to God, and God with God, and together with the Holy Spirit, one God.

How you have loved us, good Father, who spared not your only Son, but delivered him up for us wicked ones! How you have loved us, for whom he *did not count it robbery to be equal with you, but became obedient unto death, even the death of the cross*! He alone was free among the dead, having power to lay down his life and power to take it up again. For us he was both Victor and Victim, Victor because he was the Victim.

He was Priest and Sacrifice for us, and Priest because he was Sacrifice, making us sons to you instead of slaves, by being born himself your Son [in his incarnation], and becoming our slave. Rightly, then, is my hope strongly fixed in him that you will heal all my infirmities by him who *sits at your right hand and makes intercession for us.* Otherwise I should despair. For many and great are my infirmities, many they are and great! But your medicine is greater. We might think that your Word was far from any union with mankind, and despair of ourselves if he had not been made flesh and dwelt among us.

Terrified by my sins and the load of my misery, I had resolved in my heart and had purposed to flee into the wilderness. But you forbade me and strengthened me, saying, *Since Christ died for all, they who live should no longer live unto themselves but unto him who died for them.* See, Lord, I cast all my care upon you, that I may live and *behold wondrous things out of your law.* You know my unskillfulness and my infirmities: teach me and heal me. He, your only Son, *in whom are hid all the treasures of wisdom and knowledge,* has redeemed me with his blood. Let not the proud speak evil of me, because I consider my ransom, and eat and drink and minister it to others. And being poor, I desire to be satisfied with that Food together with those who eat and are satisfied. And *they that seek him shall praise the Lord.*

ST. TERESA OF AVILA

From *The Way of Perfection*

CHAPTER 6
Perfect Love

Let us now continue talking about the love that it is good for us to feel. I have described such love as purely spiritual. I am not sure what I am talking about, but it seems to me that there is no need to speak much about this kind of love, since so few, I'm afraid, possess it. If the Lord has given such love to any of you, praise him fervently, for you must be a person of the greatest perfection. Perhaps what I say may help some, for if you see a virtue, you desire it and try to gain it and become attached to it.

God grant that I may be able to understand this and be able to describe it, for I am not sure I know when love is spiritual and when there is sensuality mingled with it. I am like one who hears a person speaking in the distance and cannot understand his words. It is just like that with me: sometimes I cannot understand what I am saying, yet the Lord helps me to say it well. If at other times what I say does not make sense, it is only natural for me to go completely astray.

It seems to me that one loves very differently from others when one has learned the great difference between this world and the other one. This world is only a dream and the other is eternal. One who knows the difference between loving the Creator and loving the creature also knows the difference between purely spiritual love and spiritual love mingled with sensuality. Those who have devoted themselves to being taught by God in prayer also love very differently from those who lack such devotion.

You may think it is irrelevant for me to talk about this, and you may say you already know everything I will say. God grant this may be so. If you know it, you will see that I am telling the truth when I say that the person the Lord brings this far does indeed possess this love. Those whom God brings to this state are generous souls. They are not content with loving anything so miserable as these bodies, no matter how beautiful the bodies are nor how much grace they have. If the sight of the body gives them pleasure, they praise the Creator. But they do not have love for the body for more than a moment. If they did have such love, they would think they were loving something insubstantial and developing fondness for a shadow. They would be ashamed of themselves and would not have the courage to tell God they love him without feeling very confused.

You will say that such people cannot love or repay affection they are shown by others. Indeed, they care very little for this affection. They may experience a natural and momentary pleasure at being loved. As soon as they return to their normal condition, though, they realize that such pleasure is foolish, except when the persons concerned can benefit their souls by instruction or prayer. Any other kind of affection wearies them, for they know it cannot help them and may even harm them. Nevertheless, they are grateful for such affection and repay it by commending to God the ones who love them. Since they can see nothing lovable in themselves, they suppose the love comes from God and think that others love them because God loves them. So, they ask Christ to repay them for this, thus feeling that they have no more responsibility. I think this desire for affection is sometimes sheer blindness, except when it concerns people who can lead us to do good so we may gain blessings in perfection.

I should add here that when we desire anyone's affection we always seek it because of some interest, profit, or pleasure of our own. Those who are perfect, though, have trampled all these things beneath their feet. They have so despised this world's pleasures, delights, and blessings that they could not love anything outside God or unless it has to do with God. What can they gain, then, from being loved themselves?

When they think about the matter this way, they laugh at themselves for being so anxious in the past about whether or not their affection was being returned. No matter how pure our affection might be, though, it is quite natural for us to wish it to be returned. But the return of affection is insubstantial, like straw, as light as air and easily carried away by the wind. For, however dearly we have been loved, what is left for us? Such people, except for the advantage affection might bring to their souls (because they realize that it is in our nature soon to tire of life without love) do not care whether or not they are loved. Do you think that such people will love no one and delight in no one except God? No; they will love others much more than they did, with a more genuine love, with greater passion and with a love that brings more gain. In brief, that is what love really is. Such souls are much fonder of giving than receiving, even in their relations with God. This holy affection deserves the name of love, although the name of love has been stolen from it by those other base affections.

Yet, what attracts them if they do not love the things they see? They do love what they see and they are greatly attracted by what they hear, but the things they see are everlasting. If they love anyone, they immediately look right beyond the body, fix their eyes on the soul and see what there is to be loved in that. If there is nothing, but they see any suggestion that if they dig deep they will find gold within this mine, they will think nothing of the work of digging. They are doing this because of their love. They will do anything for the good of that soul since they want their love to be lasting. They know quite well that this is impossible unless the loved one has certain good qualities and a great love for God. Even if that soul were to die for them and perform all the kind actions in its power, this would be impossible. Even if the soul had all the natural graces joined in one, their wills would not be strong enough to love it or to remain fixed upon it. They have experienced all this and recognize its truth. They see that they are not in unison with that soul and that their love for it cannot possibly last. Unless that soul keeps the law of God, their love will end with life. They know that unless it loves him that they will go to different places.

Those into whose souls the Lord has already infused true wisdom do not value this love, which lasts only on earth, for more than it is worth. Those who take pleasure in worldly things, delights, honors, and riches will judge it of some value if their friend is rich and can afford to bring them worldly pleasures. Those who already hate all this will care little or nothing for such things. If they have any love for such a person, it will be a passion that he may love God so as to be loved by God. They know that no other kind of affection can last and that this kind will cost them dearly. For this reason they do all they possibly can for the good of their friend. They would lose a thousand lives to bring him a small blessing. Oh precious love, forever imitating the Captain of Love, Jesus, our Good!

CHAPTER 7
Spiritual Love and Some Advice on How to Achieve It

It is strange to see how much passion this love provokes. It costs many tears, penances, and prayers. The loving soul is careful to commend the object of its affection to all who it thinks may prevail with God and to ask them to intercede with him for this object of affection. The loving soul's longing is constant, and it cannot be happy unless it sees that its loved one is making progress. If the latter seems to have advanced and then falls back, her friend seems to have no pleasure in life. She does not eat or sleep and is always afraid that the soul whom she loves so much may be lost, and that the two may be parted forever. She is not concerned about physical death, but she cannot bear to be attached to something that a puff of wind may suddenly carry away. This is love without any degree of self-interest. All that this soul wishes is to see the soul it loves enriched with blessings from heaven. This is love that grows to be more like Christ's love for us. It deserves the name of love and is quite different from our petty and frivolous earthly affections.

These last affections are indeed a hell. It is needless for us to bother ourselves by saying how evil they are, for the least of the evils they bring are terrible beyond belief. We do not need ever to take such things to our lips, or even think of them, or to remember that they exist anywhere in the world. Do not ever listen to anyone speaking of such affections, either seriously or humorously, and do not allow them to be mentioned or discussed in your presence. No good can come from our discussing these affections, and it might do us harm even to hear them mentioned. But it is different regarding the lawful affections we have for each other and for relatives and friends. Our whole desire is that they should not die. If their heads ache, our souls seem to ache too. If we see them in distress, we are unable to sit still and watch it.

This is not the case with spiritual affection. Although our weak natures will at first allow us to feel sympathy for our friends, our reason soon begins to ponder whether or not our friend's trials are good for her. We wonder if these trials are making her more virtuous and how she is bearing them. Then we will ask God to give her patience for enduring trials that lead her to virtue. If we see she is being patient, we are not worried. Indeed, we are joyous and relieved. Even if she could be given all the rewards and gain that suffering is capable of producing, we would still prefer suffering ourselves to seeing her suffer. However, we are not worried or upset.

I repeat that this love is just like the love that Jesus, the good Lover, bore for us. It brings us such immense benefits, for it makes us embrace every kind of suffering, so that others, without having to endure the suffering, may gain its advantage. The recipients of such friendship gain much. Their friends should realize, however, that this exclusive friendship must come to an end or that they must pray fervently to God that their friend may walk in the same way as themselves, as Saint Monica did with him for Saint Augustine. Their heart does not allow them to be false. If they see their friend straying from the road, they will speak to her about it. They cannot allow themselves to do anything else. After this, if the loved one does not change her ways, they will not flatter her or hide anything from her. Either she will change her ways or their friendship is over. Otherwise, they would be unable to endure it, for it would mean continual war for both parties. A person may be indifferent to all other people in the world and not worry whether or not they are serving God, since the person she has to worry about is herself. She cannot feel this way about her friends. Nothing they do can be hidden from her. She sees the smallest fault in them. This is a very heavy cross for her to bear.

Happy are the souls that are loved by such as these. Happy the day on which they came to know them. O my Lord, will you grant me the favor of giving me many who have such love for me? Truly, Lord, I would rather be loved by these than by all the kings of the world, for such friends use every means in their power to give us dominion over the whole world and to have all that is in the world subject to us. Love such persons as much as you like. There can be very few of them, but it is the Lord's will that their goodness should be known. When you are striving for perfection, you will be told that you don't need to know such people; it is enough for you to know God. But, to get to know God's friends is a very good way of getting to know him. As God is my witness, it is because of such people that I am not in hell. I was always very fond of asking them to commend me to God, and I prevailed upon them to do so.

It is this kind of love that I would like us to have. It may not be perfect at first, but the Lord will make it increasingly perfect. At first it may be mingled with emotion, but, as a rule, this will do no harm. It is sometimes good and necessary for us to feel and show emotion in our love and to be distressed by some of our friends' trials and weaknesses, however trivial. For on one occasion a small matter might cause as much distress as a great trial might cause on another occasion. There are people whose nature is very much affected by small things. If you are not like this, do not neglect to have compassion on others. It may be that Our Lord wishes to spare us these sufferings and give us sufferings of another kind that will seem heavy to us, though to others they may seem light. In these matters, we must not judge others by ourselves nor think of ourselves at some time when the Lord has made us stronger than they. Let us think about what we were like at the times when we have been the weakest.

We must try hard to recall what we were like when we were weak and remember that, if we are no longer weak, it is not our doing. Otherwise, little by little, the devil could easily cool our charity toward our neighbors and make us think that what is really a failing on our part is perfection. In every respect we must be careful and alert, for the devil never sleeps. The nearer we are to perfection, the more careful we must be, since his temptations are then much more cunning. If we are not cautious, the harm is done before we realize it. We must always pray and watch, for there is no better way than prayer of revealing those hidden wiles of the devil and making him declare his presence.

It is a very good thing for us to take compassion on each other's needs. Get to know the things in others that you would be sorry to see and those about which you should sympathize with them. Always show your grief at any of their obvious faults. It is a good proof and test of our love if we can bear with such faults and not be shocked by them. Others, in their turn, will bear with your faults, which, if you include those of which you are not aware, must be much more numerous. Commend to God often any friend who is at fault and strive on your own part to practice with perfection the virtue that is opposite of her fault. Make determined efforts to do this so that you may teach by actions what your friends could never learn by words nor gain through suffering.

The habit of performing some conspicuously virtuous action through seeing it performed by another is one that easily takes root. This is good advice: do not forget it. The love of someone who can bring gain to everyone by sacrificing her own gain is true and genuine. She will make a great advance in each of the virtues. This will be a much truer kind of friendship than one that uses every possible loving expression. Keep phrases like "My life!" "My love!" and "My darling!" for your Spouse, for you will be so often alone with him that you will want to use them all. If you use them among yourselves, they will not move the Lord so much.

If you should be cross with one another because of some hasty word, you must at once correct the matter and pray earnestly. The same applies to the harboring of any grudge or to the desire to be the greatest. If this should happen to you, consider yourselves lost. Just reflect and realize that you have driven your Spouse from his home. He will have to go and seek another abode, since you are driving him from his own house. Cry aloud to Christ and try to correct things.

CHAPTER 8
The Benefits of Detachment from
all Earthly Things

We must practice detachment, for if we perform it perfectly it includes everything else. If we do not concern ourselves with created things, but embrace the Creator alone, God will infuse the virtues into us in such a way that we will not have to wage war much longer. The Lord will defend us from the devils and the whole world. Do you think, daughters, that it is a small benefit to get for ourselves this blessing of giving ourselves entirely to him and of keeping nothing for ourselves? Since all blessings are in him, let us praise him heartily for having brought us together here. I do not know why I am saying this, when all of you here are capable of teaching me. I confess that, in this important respect, I am not as perfect as I should like to be. I must say the same about all the virtues and about all I am dealing with here, for it is easier to write about such things than to practice them.

As far as exterior matters are concerned, you know how completely cut off we are from everything. Oh, sisters, for the love of God, try to recognize the great favor the Lord has bestowed on those of us he has brought here. Let each of you apply this to herself, since there are only twelve of us and God has been pleased for you to be one. I know many people who are better than I who would gladly take my place, yet the Lord has granted it to me who so poorly deserves it. Blessed be you, my God, and let the angels and all created things praise you, for I cannot repay this favor any better than I can repay any of the others you have given me. It was a wonderful thing to call me to be a nun. But, I have been so wicked, Lord, that you could not trust me. In a place where there were many good women living together, my wickedness might have gone unnoticed. Indeed, I did conceal it from you for many years. But, you brought me here, where there are so few of us that my wickedness is impossible not to notice. You remove occasions of sin from me so that I may walk more carefully. There is no excuse for me, then, O Lord, I confess it, and so I need your mercy so you may forgive me.

What I earnestly beg of you is that anyone who knows she will be unable to follow our customs will say so before she enters our community. There are other convents where the Lord is also well served, and she should not stay here and disturb these few of us whom God has brought together for his service. In other convents nuns are free to have the pleasure of seeing their relatives. Here, if relatives are ever admitted, it is for their own pleasure. A nun who wishes to see her relatives in order to see herself must, unless they are spiritual people and do her soul some good, consider herself imperfect and realize she is neither detached or perfect. She will have no freedom of spirit or perfect peace. If she does not lose this desire, she is not intended for this house.

The best remedy is that she should not see her relatives again until she feels free in spirit and has gained this freedom from God through many prayers. When she considers such visits as crosses to bear, let her receive them, for then the visits will do the visitors good and do her no harm. However, if she is fond of the visitors, if their troubles distress her greatly, and if she delights in listening to their stories about the world, she may be sure that she will do herself harm and do the visitors no good.

CHAPTER 9

Why We Must Avoid Our Families and How We Can Find Our True Spiritual Friends

If we religious only understood how much harm comes from having so much to do with our relatives, how we would shun them. I do not see what pleasure they can give us or how they can bring us any peace or tranquility. For we cannot take part in their pleasures, since it is not lawful for us to do so. Though we can certainly share their troubles, we can never help weeping for them, sometimes more than they do themselves. If they bring us any bodily comforts, we will pay for it in our spiritual lives and our poor souls. But, you are free from that here. You have everything in common, and none of you may accept any private gift. The community holds all the offerings given to us. You are under no obligation to entertain your relatives in return for what they give you. The Lord will provide for all of us in common.

I do not know how much of the world we really leave when we say we are leaving everything for God's sake if we do not withdraw ourselves from the chief worldly thing—our relatives. The matter has become so serious that some people think that religious must lack virtue if they are not fond of their relatives or see them very much.

In this house, daughters, we must commend our relatives to God, for that is only right. In all other matters, we must keep them out of our minds as much as we can. It is natural, after all, that our desires be attached to them more than to other people. My own relatives were very fond of me, and I was so fond of them that I would not let them forget me. But I have learned through experience that it is God's servants who have helped me in trouble. My relatives, except for my parents, have not helped me very much. Parents are different, for they very rarely fail to help their children. It is right that when they need our comfort we should not refuse them. If we find that doing so does not harm our main purpose, we can give them help and remain completely detached.

Believe me, sisters, if you serve God as you should, then you will find no better relatives than those servants of God that he sends to you. If you keep on doing as you are doing here, and realize that by doing otherwise you will be failing your true Friend and Spouse, you will soon gain this freedom. Then you will be able to trust those who love you for his sake alone more than all your relatives. They will not fail you. You will find parents, brothers, and sisters where you least expected to find them. These people help us and look for their reward only from God. Those who look for rewards from us soon grow tired of helping us when they see we are poor and can do nothing for them.

All the advice the saints give us about withdrawing from the world is good. Attachment to our relatives is the thing that sticks to us most closely and is hardest to get rid of. People are right, then, to withdraw from their own part of the country, if it helps them. For I do not think it helps us so much to leave a physical place as to embrace the good Jesus, Our Lord, with the soul. Just as we find everything in him, so for his sake we forget everything. Until we have learned this truth, though, it helps us to keep apart from our relatives. Later on, the Lord might want us to see them again so that what used to give us pleasure may be a cross to us.

CHAPTER 10
How to Attain the Virtue of
Self-Detachment and Humility

O nce we have detached ourselves from the world and are
cloistered here without any possessions, it must look
as if we have done everything and there is nothing left with
which we must contend. But, my sisters, do not feel secure
and fall asleep, or you will be like the person who bolted all
her doors for fear of thieves only to find that the thieves were
already in the house. Unless we take great care and each of us
renounces her self-will, many things will deprive us of that
holy freedom of spirit that allows our souls to soar to their
Maker unburdened by the earth's heavy weight.

If we keep the vanity of all things constantly in our
thoughts, we will be able to withdraw our affections from
trivial things and fix them on eternal things. This may seem
poor advice but it will fortify the soul greatly. We must be
very careful, for as soon as we begin to grow fond of small
things we must withdraw our thoughts from them and turn
our thoughts to God. He has granted us the great favor of
providing that, in this house, most of it is done already. But
we must become detached from ourselves. It is difficult to
withdraw from ourselves and oppose ourselves, because we
are very close to ourselves and love ourselves very dearly.

This is where true humility can enter. True humility and
detachment from self always go together. You must embrace
them, love them, and never be seen without them. Oh, how
sovereign are these virtues—mistresses of all created things,

empresses of the world, our deliverers from the devil's snares—that our Teacher, Christ, so dearly loved and who was never without them. The one who possesses them can safely go out and fight all the united forces of hell and the whole world and its temptations. This person does not need to fear anyone, for hers is the kingdom of the heavens. She does not care if she loses everything; her sole fear is that she may displease God, and she begs him to nourish these virtues within her so she will not lose them through any fault of her own.

These virtues are hidden from the one who possesses them, even if she is told that she has them. She prizes them so much, though, that she is always trying to obtain them. She thus perfects them more and more in herself. Those who possess them soon make the fact clear to anybody with whom they have contact. How inappropriate it is for me to begin to praise humility and sacrifice when these virtues are so highly praised by the King of Glory, a praise exemplified in all the trials he suffered. You must work to possess these virtues, my daughters, if you are to leave the land of Egypt. For when you have attained these virtues, you will also attain the manna. All things will taste good to you, and no matter how much the world may dislike their savor, to you they will be sweet.

We must first rid ourselves immediately of our love for our bodies. Some of us pamper ourselves so much that doing so will be hard work. It is also amazing how concerned some of us are about having a healthy body. Some of us think, though, that we embraced the religious life for no other reason than to keep ourselves alive. In our community, there is very little chance for us to act on such a principle. We have come here to die for Christ, not to practice self-indulgence for Christ. The devil tells us that we need to be self-indulgent if we are to keep the Rule of our Order. So many of us try to keep the Rule by looking after our health that we die without having kept it for even a day.

It is really amusing to see how some people torture themselves for their excessive behavior, for the real weakness in their souls. Sometimes they perform penances without any reason. They perform them for a few days and then the devil puts it into their heads that they have been doing themselves harm and makes them afraid of penances. After this they don't even do what the Order requires. They do not keep the smallest points in the Rule, such as silence, which is quite incapable of harming them. If we imagine we have a headache, we stay away from choir. One day we are absent because we had a headache some time ago. Another day we are absent because our head has just begun to ache again. We are absent the next three days in case it aches any more. Then we want to invent penances on our own, and we end up doing neither one thing nor the other. Sometimes there is very little wrong with us, but we think it should release us from all our obligations.

Oh, God help me! that nuns should be complaining so much. May he forgive me, but I am afraid such complaining has become quite a habit. A nun began complaining to me about her headaches and went on complaining for a long time. When I questioned her about her pain, I found she did not have a headache at all but that she was suffering from some pain in another part of her body.

These are things that might sometimes happen, and I write about them so you may be on guard against them. If the devil begins to frighten us about losing our health, we will never get anywhere. May the Lord give us light so that we may act rightly in everything.

CHAPTER 11

On Self-Sacrifice and How to Attain
It Even in Times of Sickness

This continual moaning about trivial illnesses seems to me a sign of imperfection. If you can bear something, do not talk about it. A serious illness will draw attention to itself. Remember, there are only a few of you. If one of you gets into this habit, she will worry all the rest, assuming you love each other and there is charity among you. On the other hand, if one of you is really ill, she should say so and take the necessary medicine. If you have put aside your self-love, you will so regret indulging yourselves in any way that you will be afraid of self-indulgence without a proper cause. When such a reason does exist, it would be much worse to say nothing about it than to allow yourselves unnecessary indulgence. It would also be wrong if others were not sorry for you.

I am quite sure that if there is prayer and charity among you that you will always be taken care of. Do not complain about the weaknesses and minor ailments that women suffer, for the devil sometimes makes you imagine them. They come and go; unless you get out of the habit of talking and complaining about minor illnesses, they will always bother you. Our body has one fault: the more you indulge it, the more things it discovers that it has to have. It is extraordinary how the body likes to be indulged. If there is any reasonable pretext for indulgence, no matter how unnecessary it is, the poor soul is taken in and prevented from making progress. Think about how many poor people must be ill and have no one to complain to. Poverty and self-indulgence make bad company. Surely we have not come here to indulge ourselves more than they. You are free from the great trials of the world. Learn to suffer a little for the love of God without telling everyone about it. When a woman has made an unhappy marriage she does not talk about it or complain, for she does not want her husband to know. She has to endure a great deal of misery and she has no one to whom she may talk. Can't we, then, keep secret between God and us some of the afflictions he sends us because of our sins? Even more so, for talking about them does not help to lessen them.

I am not referring to serious illnesses, though with these, too, I ask you to observe moderation and to have patience. I am thinking of those minor afflictions that you might have. When afflicted in such a way, you can go about your daily offices without worrying everybody else about them. When there is one person who talks continually about her minor illnesses, it often happens that some suffer on account of others and others will not believe her when she says she is ill, no matter how serious her sickness might be. Let us remember our holy Fathers, the hermits whose lives we strive to imitate. What sufferings, solitude, cold, and burning heat, and hunger and thirst they bore. Yet they had no one to complain to except God. Do you think they were made of iron? They were as frail as we are. Once we begin to subdue these miserable bodies of ours, they give us much less trouble. There will be plenty of people to see to what you really need. Do not think about yourselves except when you know it is necessary. Unless we resolve to endure illness and death once and for all, we will never accomplish anything.

Try not to fear illness and death and commit yourselves to God. What does it matter if we die? How many times have our bodies ridiculed us? Shouldn't we occasionally ridicule them? If we make this resolution day by day, by the grace of the Lord we will be able to control our body. To conquer such an enemy is a great achievement in the battle of life. May the Lord grant, as he is able, that we may do this. I am quite sure that everyone who enjoys such a victory, which I believe is a great one, will understand the advantages it brings. No one will regret having endured trials in order to attain this tranquility and self-mastery.

CHAPTER 12
Why the True Lover of God Must Not
Care About Life and Honor

There are some other little things we need to talk about, though they will appear trivial. This seems to be a great task, for it involves battling against ourselves. But once we begin to work, God works in our souls and bestows such favors on them that the most we can do in this life does not seem like very much. We are doing everything we can by giving up our freedom for the love of God and entrusting it to one another. We are doing our best to serve God by putting up with so many trials—fasts, silence, service in choir—that no matter how much we want to indulge ourselves we can only do so occasionally. In all the convents I have seen, I am the only nun guilty of self-indulgence. Why, then, do we shy away from interior sacrifice when it is the means by which every other kind of sacrifice can be practiced with greater tranquility and ease and with greater reward? We can acquire such self-sacrifice by gradual progress and by never indulging our will and desire, even in small things, and succeed in subduing the body to the spirit.

This consists entirely in our ceasing to care about ourselves and our own pleasures, for the least that anyone who is beginning to serve the Lord can offer him is her life. Once she has surrendered her will to him, what does she have to fear? If she is a true religious and person of prayer and strives to enjoy divine consolations, she must not turn away from the desire to die and suffer martyrdom for his sake. The life of a good religious, who wants to be among God's closest friends, is one long martyrdom. How do we know that our lives will be so short that they will end only one hour or one moment after we decide to commit our entire service to God? We must not measure ourselves by anything that comes to an end, least of all by life, since not a day of it is secure. Who, if she thought that each hour might be her last, would not spend it working for God?

It is perhaps a good thing to think this way, for by doing so we can learn to subdue our wills in everything. If you are very careful about your prayer, you will soon find yourselves gradually reaching the top of the mountain without knowing how you have done so. How harsh it sounds to say we must not take pleasure in anything. But, we must remember what consolations and delights come from this renunciation and how much we gain from it, even in this life. As you all practice such renunciation, you have done the principal part. Each of you encourages and helps the rest. Each of you must try to outstrip her sisters.

Be careful about your inner thoughts, especially if they have to do with rank. May God, by his Passion, keep us from dwelling upon such thoughts as: "But I am her senior"; "But I am older"; "But I have worked harder"; "But that other sister is being treated better than I am." If you have these thoughts, you must quickly stop them. If you allow yourselves to dwell on them, or introduce them into your conversation, they will spread like the plague and in religious houses they may give rise to great abuses. Pray fervently for God's help in this matter.

You may say that God grants consolations to people who are not completely detached from such concerns with rank and honor. In his infinite wisdom he sees that this will enable him to lead them to leave everything. By "leaving everything," I do not mean entering the religious life, for there may be obstacles to this. The perfect soul can be detached and humble anywhere. This soul will find it harder to be detached in the world, though, for worldly trappings will be an obstacle to it. Questions of honor and property can arise within convents as well as outside them. The more these kinds of temptations are removed from us, the more we are to blame if we yield to them. Though people who yield may have spent many years in prayer or meditation—for perfect prayer eventually destroys all these attachments—they will never make great progress or come to enjoy the real fruit of prayer.

Ask yourselves if these worldly things mean anything to you. The reason you are here is so that you may detach yourselves from them. You do not gain greater honor by having them, and these attachments lose you advantages that might have gained you more honor. Thus, you get both dishonor and loss at the same time. Let each of you ask herself how humble she is, and she will see how far she has come. If she is really humble, I do not think the devil will tempt her to be concerned about rank. If a humble soul is tempted by the devil in this way, her humility will bring her more courage and greater gain. Such a temptation will cause her to examine her life. It will cause her to compare the services she has given to her Lord with what she still owes him. This temptation will cause her to think over her sins, to remember where she deserves to be on account of her sins, and to recall how our Lord humiliated himself to give us an example of humility. The soul receives such great gain that Satan will not dare to come back again lest he should get his head broken.

God deliver us from people who wish to serve him yet who are overly concerned with their own honor. Reflect upon how little they gain from this. The very act of wishing for honor robs us of it, especially in matters of rank. There is no poison in the world that is so fatal to perfection. You wonder why I am concerned about what you think are trivial things. They are not trivial; in religious houses they spread like foam on water, and there is no small matter like ceremoniousness about honor and sensitivity to insult. Its root might be in some small slight, and the devil will then persuade someone else to consider it important. She will think that it is kind to tell you about the slight and ask you how you can allow yourself to be insulted. She will pray that God will give you patience and that you will offer patience to God. The devil is simply putting his deceit in the other person's mouth. Though you are quite ready to bear this slight, you are tempted to vanity because you have not resisted something else as perfectly as you should have.

Our human nature is so wretchedly weak that, even though we tell ourselves there is nothing to make a fuss about, we imagine we are being virtuous. We begin to feel sorry for ourselves, especially when we see that other people feel sorry for us, too. In this way the soul begins to lose the rewards it had gained. It becomes weaker and opens a door to the devil that he can enter with a temptation worse than the last. Even when you are prepared to suffer an insult, your sisters say you ought to be more sensitive about things. For the love of God, my sisters, do not let charity move you to show pity for others who have been the targets of these imagined insults, for such pity is like the kind that Job's wife and friends showed him.

CHAPTER 27

The First Words of the Our Father and God's Great Love

"Our Father, which art in the heavens." My Lord, how fittingly you reveal yourself as the father of such a Son. How fittingly your Son reveals himself as the Son of such a Father. May you be blessed forever and ever. Shouldn't a favor as great as this one come at the end of the prayer? Here at the beginning you fill our hands and grant us so great a favor that it would be a great blessing if our understanding could be filled and our will occupied. We would thus be unable to say another word. How appropriate perfect contemplation would be here. How right the soul would be to enter into itself, so it could rise above itself and so that this holy Son might show it the nature of the place where he says his Father dwells—in the heavens. Let us leave earth, for it is not right that such a favor should be valued so little.

How can you give us so much with your first word, O Son of God and my Lord? It is wonderful that you should descend to such a degree of humility to join with us when we pray and to become the Brother of such lowly and miserable creatures. How can you give us, in the name of your Father, all that there is to be given by willing him to have us as his children? You oblige him to fulfill his word. This is no light task since, being our Father, he must bear with us no matter how great our sins are. If we return to him, as did the prodigal son, he must pardon us. He must comfort us in our trials, and he must sustain us as such a Father is bound to do. For he is better than any earthly father, since everything has its perfection in him. He must cherish us; he must sustain us; at the last he must make us participants and fellow-heirs with you.

My Lord, with the love you have for us and with your humility, nothing can be an obstacle to you. You have lived on the earth and have clothed yourself in our humanity. You thus have a reason to care about our good. But, as you have told us, your Father is in heaven, and you should consider his honor. Since you have offered yourself to be dishonored by us, leave your Father free. Do not ask him to do so much for wicked people like me, who will be poor examples for him.

You have shown clearly that you are One with him and that your will is his and his is yours. What an open confession this is, my Lord. What is this love that you have for us? You deceived the devil by concealing from him your identity as the Son of God. Your great desire for our welfare overcomes all obstacles to your granting us this great favor. Who but you could do this, Lord? I can't understand how the devil failed to understand from your word who you were. I see clearly that you spoke both as a dearly beloved son on your behalf and on our behalf. You have such power that what you say in heaven will also be done on earth. Blessed be you forever, my Lord, who love to give so much that no obstacles can prevent you from doing so.

Don't you think our Master is good, since he begins by granting us this great favor to make us love to learn what he has to teach us? Do you think it would be right for us to stop trying to think of what we are saying while we are repeating this prayer with our lips, just because picturing such love would tear our hearts to pieces? Anyone who realized his greatness would not ask such a question. What son would not try to learn his father's identity if he had one as good as ours? If God were not all these things it would not surprise me if we did not want to be known as his children.

O College of Christ, in which the Lord was pleased that Saint Peter, a fisherman, had more authority than Saint Bartholomew, the son of a king. Our Lord knew what a fuss would be made about who was fashioned from the finer clay. Dear Lord, we make such trouble about these things. God deliver us from such arguments, even if they are carried on only in fun. I hope that our Lord will indeed deliver you. If any such strife happens among you, let the person concerned be afraid, for it is like having Judas among the Apostles. Do what you can to get rid of such a bad companion. If you cannot get rid of her, give her penances heavier than anything else until she realizes that she has not deserved to be even the basest clay. The good Jesus gives you a good Father. Strive to lead such a life that you deserve to find comfort in him and to throw yourselves into his arms. If you are good children, he will never send you away. Who would do anything they could rather than lose such a Father?

Thank God that there is great cause for comfort here. I will let you think about all these things. No matter how much your thoughts may wander between such a Son and such a Father, the Holy Spirit will come to you. May he enflame your will and bind you to himself with fervent love.

ST. FRANCIS DE SALES

From *Treatise on the Love of God*

"OUR NATURAL TENDENCY IS TO LOVE GOD"

From *Treatise on the Love of God*

CHAPTER 1
Our Natural Tendency to Love God

There is a natural attraction between God and the human soul. The slightest contemplation of the divine brings us pleasure. The tiniest sunbeam is brighter than the moon and stars at night. This delight we naturally have in God is the result of something innately given. It is undeniable, but it is not easy to understand. We are created "in the image of God" (Genesis 1:27). This makes us exceptionally attracted to the divine majesty.

This relationship brings joy to both participants. Poverty welcomes generous wealth. Generous wealth enjoys helping the poor and needy. The more we need, the more ready we are to receive. It is a good thing when wealth and poverty meet. Deciding which receives the most benefit would be difficult if Christ had not told us, "It is more blessed to give than to receive" (Acts 20:35). This indicates that God receives more pleasure in giving than we do in receiving. Sometimes a nursing mother's breasts become engorged with milk. Though her baby ravenously accepts it, the mother experiences great relief. The child is necessarily satisfying hunger. The mother gives from her abundance.

In the same way, Theotimus, we are empty and need to be filled with the divine. God's abundance doesn't really need our deficiency. It gains nothing when it pours itself out. But we need God. Our spiritual appetite cannot be satisfied by anything on earth. We naturally desire the goodness of God.

A female partridge will sometimes rob another bird's nest and brood eggs it did not lay. Is it because she wants to be a mother? Is she simply stupid? It is documented that the moment the fledglings hear their true mother's call they will desert the one who hatched and fed them. This response in the young birds is dormant, waiting for the impulse that gives it life.

We may be born and nourished in this physical world, but we have a latent, natural receptivity to the spiritual. We respond to God.

Eagles are powerful birds. Their eyes are even more remarkable than their unusually strong wings and heart. They can see far beyond where they are flying. The human soul is implanted with a natural tendency to seek God. Like the eagle, we see beyond our present location. Our perception of God can be stronger than our willingness to love God.

To put it simply, Theotimus, our fallen nature is like the palm trees that grow in temperate climates. They produce imperfect, almost experimental fruit. To produce delicious, ripe dates the trees must grow in warmer places. We are naturally inclined toward God, but we remain undeveloped. We do not ripen into total love. We experience inner stirrings, but a little imperfect love is as far as it goes. Our desire for something better has the palsy. It can see the health-giving pool of holy love, but it doesn't have the strength to get into it [John 5:1–15]. We do not prefer God above all else. The apostle cried out, "I have the desire to do what is good, but I cannot carry it out. For what I do is not the good I want to do; no, the evil I do not want to do—this I keep on doing" (Romans 7:18–19).

Have we, then, been given an attraction for something that is utterly beyond us? If we have such a thirst, is there no water to drink? The truth is very much to the contrary. Our natural desire for God can be satisfied. God uses this fondness in us as though it were a handle that one can grasp. We are like deer that royalty has collared and allowed to run free in the woods. Anyone who sees one understands by the coat of arms on the collar that it belongs to the prince.

In every human soul God implanted a desire to seek the divine. It is in you. It is in your friends. It is in your enemies. It indicates that we did not merely belong to our Creator at the beginning, but that we still belong to him. God has the right to claim us as his own. He has given us free wills and lets us go about our own business in this world, but we are his. Our happiness depends upon recognizing and acting upon this.

CHAPTER 2
How God in Christ Inspires Us to Love

The sky gives us signs of rain. We see a red sun or a dim sun and understand what it forecasts. Theotimus, the sun does not change colors. It constantly emits a bright, clear light. When we speak of a red sun or a gray sun, we are reporting how it looks to us. Its light is being filtered through varying conditions of atmosphere. This makes it seem to change color and brightness.

It is the same way when we talk about God. We use language that expresses our impressions of God's activity. Thus we say that God is merciful, just, true, omnipotent, wise, holy, infinite, immortal, and invisible. Because God is busy in a multitude of ways we give him many attributes. But God is not divided and scattered. God is unified perfection. As the sun has none of the colors we report and yet is the source of every color, God is a single perfection and the source of all that is perfect.

God is the only theologian who knows the truth about God. Not one of us can possess complete knowledge of infinite divinity and express it in words. "Why do you ask my name? It is beyond understanding" (Judges 13:18). We are simply too limited to unveil infinity. We use all the language at our disposal. What we say may be true enough. Without a doubt, God is all these things, but he is more than all these things.

"We could say much more and never finish, but it all means this: the Lord is everything. How can we find the power to praise him? He is greater than all his creation. The Lord is awesome in his greatness; his power is overwhelming. Though you do your best to praise him, he is greater than you can ever express. Though you honor him tirelessly and with all your strength, you still cannot praise him enough. No one has seen him, no one can describe him. . . . Mysteries greater than these are still unknown; we know only a fraction of his works" (Sirach 43:27–32 TEV). There is no way, Theotimus, that you will ever fully comprehend God. "God is greater than our hearts" (1 John 3:20).

GOD'S INVOLVEMENT IN OUR WORLD

God had no difficulty creating a great variety of animals. His desire was to be in communication with his creation. There was no better way to do this than to unite himself with people, to implant a little divinity. He became a part of us.

This unity reached its peak in Christ. "For by him all things were created: things in heaven and on earth, visible and invisible, whether thrones or powers or rulers or authorities; all things were created by him and for him" (Colossians 1:16). We plant a grapevine in order to get grapes. Fruit is the object of leaves and buds. Similarly, our Savior was God's first objective. When he created a universe it was like the planting of a vine. As it takes many seasons for a vineyard to come into production, so our world had to be prepared for Christ. The prophets and forerunners made things ready for him.

God does not save everyone in a general and universal way. There is great variety in the expression of his mercy. "He causes his sun to rise on the evil and the good, and sends rain on the righteous and the unrighteous" (Matthew 5:45). God attempts to reach every one of us. His seed is scattered freely, but not all of it is received well. "As he was scattering the seed, some fell along the path; it was trampled on, and the birds of the air ate it up. Some fell on rock, and when it came up, the plants withered because they had no moisture. Other seeds fell among thorns, which grew up with it and choked the plants. Still other seed fell on good soil. It came up and yielded a crop, a hundred times more than was sown" (Luke 8:5–8). God offers his grace in abundance to all of us in a great variety of ways. It is our receiving it that makes the difference.

A Variety of Spiritual Gifts

Our spiritual makeup is as varied as our physical. Each person has distinct gifts. Our diversity is infinite. "The sun has one kind of splendor, the moon another, and the stars another; and star differs from star in splendor" (1 Corinthians 15:41). So it is with people. God's grace comes in infinite variety.

It is not helpful to ask why one person is blessed in a particular way. God's "grace is sufficient" (2 Corinthians 12:9) for each one of us. Why are melons bigger than strawberries? Why do lilies grow taller than violets? Why is the rosemary not a rose or the dianthus not a marigold? Why is a peacock more glamorous than a bat? Why is a fig sweet while a lemon is acidic? These are absurd questions. The beauty of the world depends upon variety. Differences and what appear to be inequalities are essential and inescapable. This thing is not that thing.

It is the same way in the spiritual dimension. Each of us has a particular "gift from God; one has this gift, another that" (1 Corinthians 7:7). It is disrespectful to ask why St. Paul and St. Peter did not have similar gifts and abilities. The church is a garden with a great variety of plants. Each one has its value and charm. It is the combination of their colors and textures that make the garden a thing of beauty.

Jesus wants our love. "Love the Lord your God with all your heart and with all your soul and with all your mind. This is the first and greatest commandment" (Matthew 22:37–38). Think about it, Theotimus! God loves us and wants our love in return. This is not something we have to work for. A response of love is what matters. This is why God implanted this natural tendency in us.

LOVE IS LIFE

To live God's way is to love. "Anyone who does not love remains in death" (1 John 3:14). God is so eager for us to love him, issuing an open invitation to the general public is not enough. He makes house calls, going from door to door. "Here I am! I stand at the door and knock. If anyone hears my voice and opens the door, I will go in and eat with him, and he with me" (Revelation 3:20). Notice that this divine lover at the door is not content merely to knock. He stands there knocking. He calls out to the soul, "Arise, my darling, my beautiful one, and come with me" (Song 2:10). He rattles the doorknob.

"I have loved you with an everlasting love; I have drawn you with loving-kindness" (Jeremiah 31:3). Jesus said, "No one can come to me unless the Father who sent me draws him" (John 6:44).

I thought of this when I discovered that Aristotle catalogued a bird he named "footless" (apodes). Their legs are very short and their feet are virtually useless. Once they land on the ground they are not able to fly again on their own. Wind is required to get them airborne. If there is sufficient breeze they begin to flap their wings and gradually lift into the air.

We are like these poor birds. We decide to land on earth and abandon the air of divine love. It is a kind of death. We stumble about on the weak legs of our affections. We make a few feeble attempts at love, but remain unable to detach ourselves from earthly things and fly again with God.

Justice would be served if God neglected us. Only God's great love prevents this from happening. Our behavior excites divine compassion and causes God to consider ways to rescue us. Divine inspiration becomes a helpful wind that begins to lift us again. It blows with tender forcefulness. Our thinking is less tethered to earth. We begin to soar in the atmosphere of God's love.

AWAKENING LOVE

We are startled when our hearts are divinely aroused. We have nothing to do with this event. It catches us completely off guard. We are not "competent to claim anything for ourselves, but our competence comes from God" (2 Corinthians 3:5). Our souls are energized.

The princely apostle, Peter, was stunned by his behavior the night he betrayed his Master. This prevented him from even thinking about the dimension of his sin. It was as though he had never known Jesus. He was as helpless as that wretched, footless bird we read about. He was stuck in the mess he had made for himself.

Providentially, God used the crowing of a rooster as an enabling breeze. Peter heard it at the same instant he saw his Lord glancing at him from a balcony as the Romans led him along. This was an arrow of love. It changed Peter. This same kind of freeing action would take place when he was sleeping, bound with chains in Herod's well-guarded prison. "Suddenly an angel of the Lord appeared and a light shone in the cell. He struck Peter on the side and woke him up. 'Quick, get up!' he said, and the chains fell off Peter's wrists" (Acts 12:7). We are asleep in sin, Satan's prisoner and slave. Divine inspiration—like the gaze of Jesus—comes to us like a jolt in the side, waking us. This arousal takes place in us and for us, but it is not our activity. "I slept but my heart was awake. Listen! My lover is knocking" (Song 5:2). St. Bernard says it is God who utters the wakeup call. All we do is receive and respond to it. We make a serious mistake if we take any credit for our salvation.

Theotimus, we would quickly make amazing spiritual progress if we received the full impact of divine inspiration. But the flow of water from a huge and dependable spring can enter a garden only in proportion to the size of the channel through which it streams. The Holy Spirit is "a spring of water welling up to eternal life" (John 4:14). But it is not forced upon us. We must give our consent. There is a voluntary relationship between divine grace and our own will.

"As God's fellow workers we urge you not to receive God's grace in vain" (2 Corinthians 6:1). If someone who is sick extends a hand and accepts some medicine but refuses to swallow it, that medicine is wasted and useless. It is the same way when we can receive God's grace without actually receiving it. There is no result. Perhaps the sick person will take a little of the medicine, but not all of it. The result is a partial improvement. When God sends a really powerful inspiration to lead us to divine love, it is important to respond fully and not partially. This is illustrated by those good people who were invited to follow Jesus. "Lord, first let me go and bury my father" (Luke 9:59). "I will follow you, Lord; but first let me go back and say good-bye to my family" (Luke 9:61).

Brother Rufinus perceived the remarkable humility of St. Francis. He asked the saint to characterize his personal relationship with God. He replied, "I am the chief of sinners and the poorest servant of our Lord."

Brother Rufinus was astounded. He asked him how he could say such a thing when he knew many others committed sins that he had been spared.

"If God had been as merciful to them as he has been to me, no matter how bad they are, they would recognize God's gifts far better than I do and would be better servants than I am. If God deserted me I would do more evil things than anyone else."

Try to understand this, Theotimus. Francis truly believed an equal grace given by an equal mercy can be more faithfully used by one sinner than another. He was expressing his kinship with the great apostle Paul who had written, "Christ Jesus came into the world to save sinners—of whom I am the worst" (1 Timothy 1:15).

Admittedly, God sometimes pours out an incredible spiritual energy that instantly changes a wolf into a shepherd, rocks into running water, persecutors into preachers. Paul was one such recipient of a torrential outpouring from God. These are extraordinary experiences applied to only a few individuals.

God ordinarily attracts us in less dramatic ways. "I led them with cords of human kindness, with ties of love; I lifted the yoke from their neck and bent down to feed them" (Hosea 11:4). We are not drawn to God by chains about our necks like bulls or wild oxen. We are enticed. We are offered something desirable for which we have an appetite. God is a joy. He does not need to force us against our wills. He catches our attention with spiritual bait. This attraction is powerful, but our free will is not overwhelmed.

Spiritual Response

It is our business to respond to the God-given opportunity. Aristotle's footless birds spread their wings to catch the breeze. They will not go very far if they do not cooperate. If they continue to be attracted by something they see on the ground they will be stranded there. The wind will have been sent in vain. They will not have seized the opportunity to fly.

The wind that helps to lift the apodes first ruffles their feathers. These are lightweight and are easily stirred. We feel the first stirrings of God's love long before we are completely faithful to God. These are like the buds on tree limbs in the spring. The sun warms them and they swell, but they are not yet fruitful.

When St. Pachomius was a secular young man, he volunteered as a soldier in Constantine's army. Some soldiers were camped outside a little village near Thebes and could not be supplied with food. The citizens of that community were friendly Christians. They took care of the soldiers with kindness and courtesy. Pachomius was impressed. He asked for an explanation of this kindness and was told about Jesus Christ. Suddenly, God was knocking at the door to his heart. God gently called Pachomius through the warm example of these Christians. He was stirred awake. His life was utterly changed.

He was like a bird waking at dawn. It begins to stretch and hop from limb to limb. Gradually, it begins to sing more and more of its gorgeous song. The unexpected admiration Pachomius had for those Christians served as a bright ray of sunshine.

God most often works gently and gradually. He draws us nearer one step at a time. The first action is his alone. He awakens us. The remainder of the process requires our cooperation. We are not forced into service against our wills. Rather than being pulled, we are enticed.

As the process begins, we do not clearly perceive what is happening. It is like a cloudy day when we can't see the sun. A little extra brightness in the sky indicates where the sun is located, but it is hidden. We see it without really seeing it. There is not enough to allow us to say that we see it, but there is enough to keep us from saying we do not see it. This is a kind of *entrevoyons* (half-sight). This dim light of faith comes to us without argument or rational thought. It is simply present. It has enough strength to make it valid. This simple revelation does not involve evidence and experiment. An academic approach to devotion can make it plausible, but faith makes it believable. Many saw the miracles of Christ and heard him teach, without becoming faithful. They observed a persuasive argument, but they did not agree. Faith is the acceptance of the authority of the revelation.

When we step into sunshine at noon, we immediately feel the heat in addition to perceiving the light. Faith's illumination brings with it the heat of divine love. We simply know that God exists and that this good God can and will communicate with us. Such joy and pleasure! We are thrilled. "How beautiful you are, my darling! Oh, how beautiful!" (Song 1:15). This spiritual union is the ultimate delight. The soul has at last found what it desired and can rest.

We occasionally experience unanticipated internal pleasure. It comes without preparation. Often, a greater joy follows it. Oh!

I have been with the one my soul desired even before I could identify him!

"As the deer pants for streams of water, so my soul pants for you, O God. My soul thirsts for God, for the living God. When can I go and meet with God?" (Psalm 42:1–2). A falcon with its hood removed will spot its prey and begin to fly in pursuit. If it is still held by a leash it will struggle wildly. In the same way faith removes our hood of ignorance and we can see what is beyond our reach. If it were not possible to fulfill our desire, we would experience nothing but an endless torment.

There is usually a good span of time between our first awakening and complete faith. During such days we can pray the same prayer one sick boy's father prayed: "I do believe; help me overcome my unbelief!" (Mark 9:24). Expressed in other words, this prayer means, "I am no longer in darkness. My soul has seen your light. But I am not yet able to believe completely. The light is dim. Lord, help me."

CHAPTER 3
Levels of Union With God

The Council of Trent holds that there is a daily renewal and improvement of believers. Scripture supports this.

- "The path of the righteous is like the first gleam of dawn, shining ever brighter till the full light of day" (Proverbs 4:18).
- "We will in all things grow up into him who is the Head, that is, Christ" (Ephesians 4:15).
- "And this is my prayer: that your love may abound more and more in knowledge and depth of insight" (Philippians 1:9).

St. Bernard reminds us of the text that asks, "Do you not know that in a race all the runners run, but only one gets the prize?" (1 Corinthians 9:24). He tells us the prize is Jesus Christ. The only way to take hold of him is to follow him. Following Jesus will keep you moving, because Jesus continued his obedient journey to his death on the cross. St. Bernard urges us to travel with him.

Because we are on a journey, there is no limit to the development of virtue. Love is the virtue of virtues. When it has an infinite object, it becomes infinitely good. Our souls continue to grow. We can love God more each day till the end of life. "The apostles said to the Lord, 'Increase our faith!'" (Luke 17:5).

St. Paul wrote, "God is able to make all grace abound to you" (2 Corinthians 9:8). It is God, then, who gives the growth. "Whoever has will be given more, and he will have an abundance" (Matthew 13:12).

Theotimus, making honey is the chief occupation of bees, but they also make valuable wax. The loving heart will aspire to great things, but God will be pleased with smaller accomplishments as well. Little things add up.

The more we concentrate on our reflection in a mirror, the more intently our image returns its gaze. When God lovingly regards a soul created in his image, it returns the attention. Even small increases on our part open wider the path for divine love. Sacred love is not divided into the great and the small. Every aspect of it is beautiful and useful. The balm tree is aromatic in all its parts, both bark and leaves. Only love produces love. Everything about it is totally lovable.

A PARABLE

Theotimus, let me, after the manner of our Master, tell you a parable. A great king fell in love with a young princess. While he was talking with her about marriage, she collapsed as though dead. This greatly upset the king and nearly caused him to faint. She was more important to him than his own life. His love put him into action instantly. He found some extremely precious medicine in a cabinet nearby. Filling his own mouth with it, he opened her firmly set lips and teeth. Then he breathed into her mouth, pouring the cordial tonic into the princess who seemed lifeless. Gradually, she returned to her senses. He gently helped her to sit up. After a while she was able to stand on her feet. She took a few steps as he held her in his arm. With continued medication and care she began to walk alone again, holding his hand. There can be no doubt that he was lovingly caring for her. He continued to do whatever was necessary for her. If she had started to faint again, he would have caught her. If she had encountered any rough terrain that was difficult to walk, he would have supported her. He remained at her side.

The soul is our Savior's spouse. He takes it to the cabinet that contains the fragrant perfumes mentioned in the Song of Songs. When such a soul sins, it faints spiritually. It falls as though dead. Even though God is astonished by such poor choices, he rushes to help. His mercy is beyond words. He uses a stinging conscience the way the king used his medicine. The soul recovers.

God does all of this independently of our participation. As the princess may have died there on the floor if the king had not come to her assistance, the soul would remain lost to sin if God did not intervene. If the soul, regaining consciousness, consents to the assistance being offered, God will strengthen it and restore it to complete spiritual health. It goes as far as it is able. God supports and sustains it. Sometimes it limps with help. Sometimes it is carried. "By the grace of God I am what I am, and his grace to me was not without effect. No, I worked harder than all of them—yet not I, but the grace of God that was with me" (1 Corinthians 15:10).

The soul that can stand on its own feet will give glory to God. God is the source of spiritual health and strength. We live, walk, and work in God and by God. "The Lord is my shepherd, I shall lack nothing. He makes me lie down in green pastures, he leads me beside quiet waters, he restores my soul. . . . Surely goodness and love will follow me all the days of my life" (from Psalm 23).

The mother of a toddler assists her child as he needs it. She puts out her hand to catch him when he stumbles. When he is attempting to walk in a smooth, safe place, she will let him walk around a little on his own. When it is necessary, she will lend a hand or lift him in her arms. Our Lord gives us that kind of continuing care when we truly love him. He lets us walk as we will, but if we get into difficulty he helps us. "I am the Lord, your God, who takes hold of your right hand and says to you, Do not fear; I will help you" (Isaiah 41:13).

Cooperating with God allows us to endure to the end of our lives. "He who stands firm to the end will be saved" (Matthew 10:22). This is the best way. Some people may die well after a wasted life, but they arrive at port without having taken a significant voyage. Their pilgrimage is a single leap. Their enemies see them victorious without seeing them fight. God's gifts of endurance and perseverance are unknown to them. St. Bernard thinks it better if we can say, "I am convinced that neither death nor life, neither angels nor demons, neither the present nor the future, nor any powers, neither height nor depth, nor anything else in all creation, will be able to separate us from the love of God that is in Christ Jesus our Lord" (Romans 8:38–39).

At the end, we will be able to sing God's praise. "I am always with you; you hold me by my right hand. You guide me with your counsel, and afterward you will take me into glory" (Psalm 73:23–24).

None of this, of course, would be possible without the redemption that is ours because of our Lord's obedience. He "made himself nothing, but [took] the very nature of a servant, being made in human likeness. And being found in appearance as a man, he humbled himself and became obedient to death— even death on a cross!" (Philippians 2:7–8). This is the source of every grace we receive. If we will be his, Theotimus, he will be ours in glory. We have the ability to be his. It is a gift that God offers to everyone. He never denies it to anyone who willingly agrees to receive it.

Spiritual Unity

Rivers flow continuously. "All streams flow into the sea, yet the sea is never full" (Ecclesiastes 1:7). The ocean is both the source and the destination of running rivers. The only purpose of their motion is to be united with the fountain that gave them their existence. St. Augustine expressed it beautifully: "You have made us for yourself and our hearts are restless until they rest in you" (Confession 1).

Perfect union with God must wait for heaven. Here on earth we are engaged, but not married. It remains possible for us to break the engagement, but our faithful fiancé will never be disloyal. The spiritual wedding will be celebrated when we die. The love that bonds us here will become eternal.

What is the nature of this eternal union? It is extrasensory. The things we perceive in this world are limited by the capacity of our senses. The eye enjoys light, but not too much light. Pleasant music can be annoying and even painful if we are too close to its source.

Our mind's understanding of truth can be extraordinarily pleasing. But when we are lifted above natural mental processes and perceive the sacred truth of faith, we will experience unsurpassed joy. The soul will melt with pleasure.

God has signed all created things. We can trace his footsteps through the natural world. It is possible here, as it were, to see the marks of God's feet. Faith can see the very face of God, but not clearly.

We have a thirst that cannot be satisfied by the things of this world. Possessing some of the most valuable prizes here is not enough to quench our desire. Possessing too much can be suffocating. We can die of pleasure as well as grief. Alexander conquered the entire known world. Then he heard a comment that there were other nations outside his awareness. This made Alexander the Great cry like a baby who had been denied an apple. The one who was in control of more of the earth than anyone else was not satisfied. He wept for more. Is this not proof that there is not enough here to quench our thirst? Oh my soul, be restless within me. Do not allow me to be satisfied here.

A mirror contains nothing that we see in it. It is only a reflection. In the same way, faith does not hold the things it announces, but merely represents them. "Now we see but a poor reflection; then we shall see face to face. Now I know in part; then I shall know fully" (1 Corinthians 13:12).

In heaven, Theotimus, God will unite with us without any intermediary. Rather than seeing a dim reflection, we will be joined together. Our understanding will be complete.

When St. Bernard was a little boy, he fell asleep in church on Christmas. He dreamed of the virgin birth of Jesus, "like a bridegroom coming forth from his pavilion" (Psalm 19:5). This pleased him so much that he remembered the event all of his life. If a child can be so deeply struck by such a vision, imagine what it will be like when our spirits are illuminated by the light of divine glory. We will be lost in love and adoration.

An owl can see clearly at night, but it is overwhelmed by daylight. In the same way, our understanding can be educated and trained here, but even with faith it is not able to comprehend the fullness of divine essence. God will grant us a new perception in heaven. At this stage of spiritual development, divine radiance no longer blinds us. We will not be considering God from a finite distance, as we now do by faith. We will be immersed in the light of divine glory. "In your light we see light" (Psalm 36:9).

There is more in God's infinity than we will ever observe or experience. Fish can enjoy the astonishing immensity of an ocean. But no fish has ever seen it all. Birds fly through the air, but no bird has flown everywhere. Theotimus, our souls will swim in the ocean and fly in the atmosphere of divinity, but there will always remain infinitely more of God. The blessed spirits will be thrilled by two observations: the infinite beauty they contemplate and the chasm of infinity that remains to be seen.

CHAPTER 4
Risks of Loss

"If you think you are standing firm, be careful that you don't fall" (1 Corinthians 10:12). Is it possible to hold onto sacred love while navigating our way through this world? Many excellent people have suffered spiritual shipwreck. Eternal God, can it be that anyone who loves you can ever lose that love? How can anyone who has ever tasted that holy sweetness be willing to taste or swallow the bitterness of offense against you? Little children enjoy the taste of sweet milk, but resist bitter concoctions. They will cry convulsively if they are forced to swallow foul-tasting medicine.

My dear Theotimus, the heavens are "appalled at this . . . and shudder with great horror" (Jeremiah 2:12). This tells us that angels are astonished by human behavior. It is amazing to see anyone sacrifice divine love and grasp unworthy things that only bring misery.

When a full wine barrel is first tapped, it will not run unless there is a way to introduce air on top of the liquid. A barrel that is already partially drained will allow wine to flow immediately without any special venting. Our souls may have a lot of heavenly love without being full to capacity. When temptations come along, such love as we have quickly departs.

We may be very much in love with God while we are here, but this love is not absolute. Other things catch our attention. In heaven, we will be completely filled with the beauty of God. Our understanding will be utterly saturated with God. There will not be room for anything else but God. There will be no way our total awareness could be diminished.

Coral can be soft and flexible in the sea, but when it is torn from the salt water of its mother's womb and placed in the air, it becomes like a stone. Even its color changes. We are born into the sea of this world. The various currents and tides sweep us this way and that. When we finally are taken out of this place of transience, we will no longer be pushed and pulled by opposing interests and desires. We will be established firmly in eternal love.

It is not possible to see God and not love God. In this world we do not see God clearly. We catch a glimpse through the clouds of faith. We see a distorted or weak image in a mirror. Our limited knowledge leaves openings for all kinds of intruders. "Little foxes . . . ruin the vineyards, our vineyards that are in bloom" (Song 21:15).

God criticized the church in Ephesus. "I hold this against you: You have forsaken your first love" (Revelation 2:4). This does not mean they did not love God, but that their love had declined. It was no longer a growing love. It was not as fruitful as it used to be.

CHOICES

Temptations are a normal part of life. They can be dangerous. Pigeons sometimes put on an aerial display. As they fly around they make a beautiful sight, but falcons spot them and prey on them. Theotimus, it is when we amuse ourselves with momentary pleasures, instead of sticking to a direct course with God, that we get into trouble.

God does not spare us temptations. Why? Because they are an excellent spiritual exercise. They give the soul a workout. Keep in mind that "all that is in the world—the desire of the flesh, the desire of the eyes, the pride in riches—comes not from the Father but from the world" (1 John 2:16 NRSV).

When we become disordered by passions, heavenly love is not able to live in us. If love does not rule, it vanishes. It may grow in us by degrees, but it is lost quickly. If we lose the smallest part of it, we lose it all. It is like a sculpture that Phidias created long ago at Athens. It was a large ivory statue of Minerva. She held a shield upon which Phidias had carved battle scenes. One of the figures was a self-portrait of the artist. Aristotle reports that this little figure had been placed in a critical position. If anyone attempted to remove the representation of Phidias, the entire statue would crumble.

Don't blame God for your loss. You are the one responsible. It has nothing to do with the breakdown of divine assistance or grace. "God desires everyone to be saved and to come to the knowledge of the truth" (1 Timothy 2:4 NRSV). God never forsakes us. We forsake God.

Our Savior is "the true light that gives light" (John 1:9) to all of us. One day at noon a group of travelers took a nap under a shade tree. They slept deeply because they were tired and the location was cool. Eventually, the advancing sun moved the shade and put its full light on their closed eyelids. They could see the light through their closed eyes. It gently, but forcibly, awakened them. Some of them got up and began to prepare for the remainder of their journey. Others turned their backs to the sun, pulled their hats down over their eyes, and went back to sleep. Night had fallen when they finally woke up. Because they still needed to complete their trip, they attempted to travel in the dark. They strayed in various directions through the forest, in danger from wild animals.

I ask you, Theotimus, shouldn't those who arrived safely give thanks for the assistance of the sun? It did them a good turn. Its heat and light lovingly invited them to continue their journey. In contrast, the others resisted the sun's invitation. They have no right to cry in the woods. It would be absurd for them to complain, "We didn't do anything to offend the sun. Why did it not shine on us the same way it did on our companions? Why are we left to wander in this darkness?" Is there anything the sun could have done for them that it did not? It shined in equal degree upon both groups. It approached all of them with the same light. The same rays fell upon everyone. They saw the others departing and chose to turn their backs. They did not make use of the light they were given.

We are all pilgrims here. Most of us have chosen to sleep in sin. God shines all the light we need upon us. Inspirations come like sunbeams, warming us with attractive love. The question we must ask is why so few respond to God's love. We will not listen to the songs of woe of those who decide to continue their sinful sleeping. Their grief has no justification. The only complaint they have is against themselves. They are their own worst enemies.

Divine Gifts

What was your part in all of this? You consented. That's all. You did not resist God. But God began the process. The Apostle Paul asks, "What do you have that you did not receive? And if you did receive it, why do you boast as though you did not?" (1 Corinthians 4:7). Are you proud of your progress in the love of God? You didn't have it in you to remedy your situation. The infinitely good God helped you. You were asleep in your sin. You would never even have noticed God's goodness unless God took the initiative. You had no positive thought of God. Your action was the result of God's action. You merely cooperated with God, and your willingness worked in unison with God's grace. It was God who gave you the ability to cooperate.

It is folly to think that you share any fragment of the glory of your personal conversion because you did not resist it. This is the insanity of robbers and tyrants who imagine they give life to those they spare. We can obstruct the results of inspiration, but we cannot give it any. It would be foolish of the princess in the parable mentioned above to contend that she gave potency to the medicines she received. She did not cure herself. If the king had not poured them into her, she would not have had a chance. It is true that she might have resisted. She could have spat out the medicine. But there was nothing she could have done to give the medicine its power and effectiveness.

We have the fruits of God's love. The honor and praise belong to God. Since we are nothing apart from God's grace, we should be nothing except for his glory.

"Oh, the depth of the riches of the wisdom of God! How unsearchable his judgments, and his paths beyond tracing out! Who has known the mind of the Lord? Or who has been his counselor?" (Romans 11:33–34). God's wisdom exceeds our wisdom. It is pointless for us to ask why God does a certain thing. God keeps secrets in order to keep our understanding humble.

St. Augustine teaches this truth in numerous passages. He insists that no one comes to Jesus unless God draws that person to Jesus. Why one is chosen and another is not is an unanswerable question. We will never know. God's choices are not unjust because they are hidden from our understanding. "Who indeed are you, a human being, to argue with God? Will what is molded say to the one who molds it, 'Why have you made me like this?' Has the potter no right over the clay, to make out of the same lump one object for special use and another for ordinary use?" (Romans 9:20–21 NRSV). God's judgments are hidden and incomprehensible.

LOVE'S PROGENY

When a soul is deprived of the presence of divine love, little traces of it remain. One who has worked hard at preaching may dream of preaching. Love imprints in us an ability to love that lingers. As a student, in a village near Paris I discovered a well that produced an echo. It would repeat several times the words I spoke into it. A dim-witted person might have suspected there was someone at the bottom of the well who did this. I understood the echo was returned from cavities down there that collected the sound of my voice and returned it. This second voice was then gathered and redirected by a third and a fourth. Altogether, I could count eleven repetitions. These voices were not mine anymore. They merely resembled my voice. If I spoke a complete sentence, these echo voices would shorten what I said. I could hear only a few rapidly uttered syllables. Only the last word or two came back clearly. Rather than being the words of someone alive, they were spoken by hollow rock.

Here is my point: When divine love lives in a soul for a while it results in a second love. The second is the result of the first, but it is not the same thing. It is a human love that resembles divine love. Some are fooled by it the way the birds were misled when they tried to eat the grapes in a realistic painting by Zeuxis.

There is a great difference between divine love and the human love it produces in us. Divine love pronounces all the syllables, makes all of God's commandments active in us. Human love skips some of them. Divine love uses human love to accomplish its purpose. Human love alone is not as reliable. Elijah's staff performed no miracles in someone else's hand.

Those who manufacture perfume carry the scent around with them for a long time after they leave their shops. The odor of a deer is easily detected in the grass where it recently slept. Anyone who has been exposed to divine love will exude the scent of it for a while. Eventually it wears off.

This imperfect human love is good, but it is dangerous. We might think it is actually divine love. Deceiving ourselves, we imagine we are holy.

CHAPTER 5
Two Dimensions of Holy Love

L ove is the turning of the heart toward good with a willingness to please. This friendly desire to comply is the
primary motivator of love.

Here is how it operates: Faith holds that divinity is an abyss of
flawlessness beyond our comprehension. We meditate upon this
truth. We consider the multifaceted vastness of God. When we
give rapt attention to God's greatness, we naturally want to please
God. Our desire to comply with God's will becomes strong.
There is a rush of gracious affability.

Our warm, cheerful response to the goodness we see in
God results in a compliant love. We are more pleased with
pleasing God than pleasing ourselves. This is the love that
gives depth to the saints. "I have said to the Lord, 'You are
my Lord; apart from you I have no good thing'" (Psalm
16:2). "God is the strength of my heart and my portion forever" (Psalm 73:26). We embrace God. God is the source of
our pleasure. There is a spiritual affinity. The soul is filled
with the goodness of God.

We will be filled with great joy in heaven, Theotimus,
when we actually see the object of our love as a limitless
ocean of excellence and kindness. We will be like deer that
have been chased by hounds, pausing to refresh themselves
by putting their mouths into a stream of cool, clear water.

Love gives without losing anything. When we increase in
the things of God, God is not diminished. As light fills the
air, the sun is no less bright. We can become as lovely as the
things we love. This is how St. Paul expresses it: "I have been

crucified with Christ and I no longer live, but Christ lives in me" (Galatians 2:20).

This divine love is in us, but it remains fully in God. We enjoy the things of God as though they were our own. The fleece Gideon placed on dry ground filled with dew. "He squeezed the fleece and wrung out the dew—a bowlful of water" (Judges 6:38). The dew belongs to the fleece because the fleece absorbs it. The fleece belongs to the dew because the dew saturates it and it receives something worthwhile from the moisture. An eagerness to please God allows us to possess God, absorbing the best from him. It also makes us belong to God. We cheerfully do what God wants.

THE PLEASURE OF LOVE

We feed upon the things we enjoy. In the French language we have a saying that someone is fed with honor or riches. "The mouth of a fool feeds on folly" (Proverbs 15:14). "'My food,' Jesus said, 'is to do the will of him who sent me'" (John 4:34). What the doctors say is true—what we enjoy nourishes.

"I have come into my garden, my sister, my bride" (Song 5:1). When the heavenly spouse enters a devout soul, he has come into his garden. He plants in this garden the loving, friendly desire to comply that nourishes us. God is pleased that we are pleased. It is a reciprocal pleasure. He plants the tree and we return the fruit.

"Your love is more delightful than wine" (Song 1:1). Divine love has an excellent taste and fragrance. It gives pleasure without excess. It intoxicates without stupefying. Rather than exciting the senses, it elevates them.

One who desires God, while being filled with God, is not looking for something remaining to be found. It is a matter of exercising affection. Instead of being a matter of gaining enjoyment, it is a matter of enhancing enjoyment. When we visit a lovely garden we begin to stroll in it. Our walking at this stage is not for the purpose of getting to the garden. We are already there. We walk now in order to enjoy the beauty of the garden. "Look to the Lord and his strength; seek his face always" (Psalm 105:4). St. Augustine tells us that love forever seeks what it has found, not to have it, but to have it always.

THE SORROW OF LOVE

Compassion is sharing the sorrow of someone we love. The misery we observe enters our own heart. That's why French calls it *miséricorde*. It is a misery of the heart (*misère de cœur*). Compassion is to be respected because it is the offspring of love.

We can see this at work in the Bible. David was in anguish because of the loss of his son. "The king was shaken. He went up to the room over the gateway and wept. As he went, he said: 'O my son Absalom! My son, my son Absalom! If only I had died instead of you—O Absalom, my son, my son!'" (2 Samuel 18:33). Consider Mary's experience when Jesus was crucified. Her love shared all his pain, anguish, suffering, and grief. When he was presented as an infant at the temple, Simeon told her, "A sword will pierce your own soul too" (Luke 2:35).

Even if we are not closely related to someone who is suffering, we experience compassion. Caesar wept over Pompeii. Job's inadequate comforters were openly distressed by the misfortune that had come to him. Our Savior wept when his friend Lazarus died. He also wept over the city of Jerusalem.

The more someone is dear to us, the more pleasure we have in that person's well-being. We enjoy seeing that individual happy. Jacob was distraught when he saw blood on Joseph's coat, but he was overcome with joy when he discovered his son was still alive. The life had gone out of Jacob's spirit; now it revived and lived again. When I think of Jesus on the Mount of Olives saying, "My soul is overwhelmed with sorrow to the point of death" (Mark 14:34), there is no way I can be without loving sorrow.

GENEROUS KINDNESS

Our love for God begins in the desire to please that we have described. It results in generous kindness. Now, there is no way we can add any goodness to God who is already perfect and complete, "immeasurably more than all we . . . imagine" (Ephesians 3:20). If it were possible to give God still more goodness, I would be eager to provide it. Generous kindness, then, creates a desire to increase our cheerful willingness to please God. We focus more on God and less on other things. Someone asked the devout Brother Giles, one of the closest friends of St. Francis, what work is most pleasing to God. He answered by chanting, "One to one." He explained this meant that we should give all our soul (which is one) to God (who is one).

A generous, kind desire to increase one's holy, friendly willingness to comply pushes all other pleasures aside. Mary Magdalene spoke with angels at Christ's empty tomb, but took no delight in the encounter. She was looking for Jesus. When she thought she saw the gardener she had no interest in him or his flowers. "Sir, if you have carried him away, tell me where you have put him, and I will get him" (John 20:15). Nothing else could distract or satisfy her. The Magi were not content with the beauty of Jerusalem, the splendor of King Herod's court, or even the brightness of the star. They were looking for a little child.

Praising God

God's goodness is above all honor and praise. All of our bene-dictions add nothing to the riches of divine goodness. When the soul understands this situation it wishes, at least, to exalt and praise God's name. Like a sacred bee, the soul flies here and there among the flowers of the attributes of God, gathering a sweet mixture that will produce a heavenly honey of expressions of praise and appreciation. The soul magnifies and glorifies the name of its well-beloved. As the soul warms in praising God, it expands and dilates. The praises increase in frequency and intensity.

Pliny reports that nightingales enjoy singing so much they will warble for two weeks, night and day. This continual practice improves their song. The better they sing, the more they like it. This increasing desire for pleasure causes them to work even harder at trilling and warbling. Their effort improves the music; the music increases their effort. They sometimes literally sing themselves to death. Their throats burst because of so much singing.

The soul ardently attempts to praise God. It is never quite satisfied with the praise it has given. This spiritual nightingale wants to perfect its melody, doing better with each new varia-tion. The more it praises, the more it enjoys praising. It never finds satisfaction. It is always aware that the praise can be better. St. Francis began to weep as he composed his love songs. Like an exhausted nightingale, exhausting respiration through the effort of aspiration, he was not able to praise God well enough to satisfy his own need.

St. Francis gave a special name to the ones who lived in his monasteries. He called them "Cicadas," because they sang praise to God. Cicadas, Theotimus, are the pipe organs of the natural world. They make enormous sound because they do not drink water through their mouths. They don't even have mouths. They live exclusively on dew, which they suck through a little tongue on their breasts. Their cries are so raucous the insects seem to be mostly voice. Those who love God are like this. According to St. Bernard, devotion is the tongue of the heart. Through it, the soul can ingest the dew of divine perfections. With it, the soul prays, praises, and sings.

David was one of the truly great spiritual cicadas. He sang, "Praise the Lord, O my soul; all my inmost being, praise his holy name" (Psalm 103:1). It is as if he had said, "I am a mystical cicada. My soul, my thoughts, all my personal attributes are organ pipes. Let them continually praise God." One of his songs expresses this beautifully. "I will extol the Lord at all times; his praise will always be on my lips. My soul will boast in the Lord; let the afflicted hear and rejoice. Glorify the Lord with me; let us exalt his name together" (Psalm 34:1–3).

After the soul has inadequately praised God to the best of its ability, it may invite other creatures to join in a chorus. "Glorify the Lord with me; let us exalt his name together" (Psalm 34:3). The Psalmist is overcome with a holy passion that scatters his thoughts widely. He leaps from heaven to earth and then back to heaven again.

Praise the Lord.
Praise God in his sanctuary; praise him in his mighty
heavens.
Praise him for his acts of power; praise him for his surpass-
ing greatness.
Praise him with the sounding of the trumpet, praise him
with the harp and lyre,
praise him with tambourine and dancing, praise him with
the strings and flute,
praise him with the clash of cymbals, praise him with
resounding cymbals.
Let everything that has breath praise the Lord.
Praise the Lord. (Psalm 150)

The great St. Francis sang his song of the sun and many other
outstanding benedictions to ask various creatures to assist his
effort. Alone, he could not sufficiently praise the dear Savior of
his soul.

The soul that is in love with God imagines how much more
glorious the music of praise will be in heaven. In heaven's
eternity all the parts blend in a gorgeous linking of progressive
movements. Alleluias ring continually from every direction.
There are loud, thundering voices as well as soft, sweet voices
that sound like harps delicately plucked by skilled players.
Alleluia! Amen! Praise God! A voice emits from the divine
throne itself, speaking to the happy souls living in paradise.
"Praise our God, all you his servants, you who fear him, both
small and great" (Revelation 19:5). An innumerable chorus
of saints responds antiphonally, "Alleluia! Praise God!" The
voice that speaks from the throne of God is a holy willingness

to comply that results in loving, generous kindness. The desire to comply with God travels from the throne to the heart. Loving kindness travels from the heart to the throne. Heaven is filled with canticles of eternal pleasure.

Two years ago I was in Milan. In a monastery of women there was one who had a voice beyond comparison. The others sang beautifully together, but became a supporting chorus to enhance and feature the perfection of this distinctive voice. It is the same with Mary's voice as she praises God. She stands out among all the others. Her praise invites her Son, our Savior, to join her. Suddenly, we are silenced. All we can do is be in awe and admire. What song does the Son sing to his Father? All the others are perfumed, but he is perfume itself. "When Isaac caught the smell of his clothes, he blessed him and said, 'Ah, the smell of my son is like the smell of a field that the LORD has blessed'" (Genesis 27:27).

If you have heard all kinds of little birds singing in the neighboring woods and then hear the masterful singing of a nightingale, you would prefer this one song above all the others. After you have enjoyed the praises of all the heavenly hosts, the exceptional praise of our Savior will stand out with distinction. The soul responds as though it has been awakened from a deep sleep. It is enraptured.

If we praise the sun for its light, the closer we lift ourselves toward it, the more worthy of praise we will find it to be. We will discover increasing brightness as we draw nearer. It is probable that the beauty of sunlight prompts the lark to sing. If this is the case then it is no surprise that the higher it flies the better it sings. When it reaches peak altitude it begins to return to earth, its song gradually diminishing. Our love of God lifts us ever higher toward divinity to add our praise to that of others. We then perceive that God is above all praise. This prompts us to sing, "Glory be to the Father, and to the Son, and to the Holy Spirit." To affirm that it is not the glory of our praises, but the eternal glory of God himself, we continue, "As it was in the beginning, is now, and ever shall be, world without end. Amen."

CHAPTER 6

Contemplation and Meditation
—Love in Prayer

Our love of God is experienced in two ways: emotional and active, affective and effective. By the first we conceive. With the second we give birth. One places God in our heart, working in us. The other lets God use our arms, working through us.

The first exercise is essentially prayer. Prayer is such a varied experience it is impossible to describe every aspect of it. This is partly because of the many different nuances of prayer. The largest obstacle is attempting to describe something spiritual in nature. Spiritual matters are extremely obscure and almost indiscernible. The best-trained hounds often lose the track of a stag. The deer doubles back, putting them on the wrong scent. It has many tricks that help it escape the baying dogs. We easily lose the scent and understanding of our own heart because of its multiplicity of motions. We are not able to follow the track.

Only God perceives and understands the turns and twists of our hearts. "O Lord, you have searched me and you know me. . . . You perceive my thoughts from afar" (Psalm 139:1–2). God does not miss any detail. Certainly, if our spirits could reconsider our actions and turn back the way we came, we would end up in a maze from which it is impossible to escape. We are not able to think what our thoughts are. It is beyond us to observe our spiritual observations. This treatise is not an easy assignment, particularly for one who is not an expert at prayer.

Prayer is more than asking God for something good. St. Bonaventure says that prayer includes every act of contemplation. St. Gregory Nazianzen and St. Chrysostom teach that prayer is conversation with God. St. Augustine and St. Damascene describe prayer as the soul ascending to God. Prayer is a discourse of the soul with God. Through prayer we speak to God and God speaks to us.

What topics do we discuss with God? What is the subject of our conversation? Theotimus, the only thing we speak of in prayer is God. What else can love mention but the beloved? Because of this, prayer and mystical theology are identical. We can label it theology because God is the object. Systematic theology, however, examines God as God. Mystical theology deals with God as supremely friendly. The former regards the Divinity of the supreme goodness; the latter the supreme goodness of the Divinity. Instead of the knowledge of God, mystical theology considers the love of God. Systematic theology produces wise scholars and learned theologians. Mystical theology leads to fervent scholars who love God—a Philotheus or a Theophilus.

It is called mystical because the conversation of prayer is secret. No words are spoken aloud. It is not overheard by anyone else. Lovers have their own language. They do not require spoken language. Prayer, mystical theology, is a conversation between an amorous soul and God.

Prayer is "hidden manna" (Revelation 2:17). It is manna because it is delicious; it is hidden because it arrives in advance of the insights of knowledge. The soul has been compared with a dove. This bird is known to seek out shady places, apart from other birds, where the only use she makes of her song is for her mate. She courts him with it in life and mourns him with it in death. In the Song of Songs, the divine lover and the heavenly spouse characterize their love as an uninterrupted conversation.

Others may exchange thoughts with them, but this does not disturb their discussion.

At the beginning of her spiritual development, St. Teresa of Avila benefited by meditating upon those moments in the Gospels when our Savior was nearly alone—in the Garden of Gethsemane or by the well in Samaria. She felt that he accepted her into his company more readily under such circumstances.

Love wants privacy. Even though lovers may have nothing secret to say, they would rather speak it in seclusion. It is quiet, intimate conversation. A name spoken in public does not have the same impact as a name whispered secretly in the ear. O God! What contrast there is between the language of the ancient lovers of God—Ignatius, Cyprian, Chrysostom, Augustine, Hilary, Ephrem, Gregory, Bernard—and the language of less affectionate modern theologians! We use some of the same words, but when they spoke them the words were fiery and sweetly perfumed. With us, the words are cold and have no scent at all.

Beyond Words

Love has little need for language. It uses the eyes, facial expressions, and sighs. Silence has a vast vocabulary. "My heart says of you, 'Seek his face!' Your face, Lord, I will seek" (Psalm 27:8). "Hear my prayer, O Lord, listen to my cry for help; be not deaf to my weeping" (Psalm 39:12). The principal exercise in mystical theology is to speak to God and to perceive God speaking inside us. In utter silence eyes speak to eyes and heart speaks to heart. Only the lovers themselves know what is being shared.

The word "meditation" is often used in Holy Scripture. It refers to dwelling on a single thought with great attention. In the first Psalm the man is blessed whose "delight is in the law of the Lord, and on his law he meditates day and night" (Psalm 1:2). On the other hand, in the second Psalm we discover that meditation can focus on evil as well as on good. "Why do the nations rage, and the people meditate on vain things?" (Psalm 2:1, paraphrased). Today, we commonly understand meditation to mean concentrated attention on the holy. This is the first degree of prayer in mystical theology.

Meditation involves thinking, but all thinking is not meditation. Our random thoughts are like flies in a flower garden. They gather no honey. If we focus our attention on such passing notions we may call it "thinking," but this is quite different from meditation. Our best study of a subject is like a locust that feeds itself by chewing on plants. The purpose of meditation is not education, but appreciation and love. Rather than satisfying an intellectual hunger, meditation visits the flowers of holy mysteries to gather divine love's honey.

It is common to daydream. Thoughts drift through our minds without any particular pattern. Intellectual curiosity leads us to dig deeply into a subject. Only a few of us meditate in order to open ourselves to God's love. Casual thinking and disciplined scholarship may get into almost any imaginable subject. Meditation centers only upon that which will help us to be devout.

Hezekiah, king of Judah, said, "I cried like a swift or thrush, I moaned like a mourning dove" (Isaiah 38:14). Have you ever noticed, dear Theotimus, that most birds sing with their beaks wide open while the dove makes its call with its beak closed? The sound seems to come from its throat and breast and emerges with a peculiar resonance and reverberation. This closed-mouth murmuring is all they need to communicate both grief and joy. Hezekiah cried out "like a swift or thrush" during his illness. His prayers were uttered aloud. He openly expressed his discomfort and fears. Then he turned to silent prayer. Quietly and privately, in his own mind, he meditated in the manner of a dove. He thought continuously about the way God mercifully restored his health. This led him to bless and praise God. As Isaiah expressed it, "We all growl like bears; we moan mournfully like doves" (Isaiah 59:11). The growling of bears is the noise we make with vocal prayer. The moaning of doves is holy meditation.

The Lord commanded Joshua, "Do not let this Book of the Law depart from your mouth; meditate on it day and night, so that you may be careful to do everything written in it" (Joshua 1:8). Prolonged meditation results in respect, determination, and activity. The best way to accomplish and fulfill the law is to keep your mind on it. The apostle gives the same guidance. "Consider him who endured such opposition from sinful men, so that you will not grow weary and lose heart" (Hebrews 12:3). Such consideration is meditation. Why does he want us to meditate upon the passion of Christ? It is not a matter of education. Instead of the learning of facts, the intended result is the gaining of patience and endurance. "Oh, how I love your law! I meditate on it all day long! (Psalm 119:97). David meditates on God's law because he loves it; he loves it because he meditates on it.

Focused Meditation

When a bee flies from one spring flower to another there is nothing random about it. The bee is not there to revel in the beauty of springtime. Its purpose is to gather honey. It loads itself with pollen. Returning to the hive, it is able to fill a wax comb with life-sustaining nourishment. This is the way it is with a devout person who meditates. Meditation is not a haphazard flitting from mystery to mystery. The point is not personal pleasure in enjoying the things of God. There is an intentional purpose to discover motivating love. She gathers what she can and stores it in her heart for use in difficult times.

In the Song of Songs the soul-spouse flits about like a mystical bee. It lands on its beloved's lips, cheek, and hair. It is attracted by the sweetness of a thousand impulses of love, observing what is most appealing. On fire with holy love, it talks with him and asks him questions. He delights it, inspires it. He pours brightness into its open heart. This is all done secretly. It might be said of this sacred conversation between the soul and God as it was said of Moses when he was alone with God on Mount Sinai: "Then Moses spoke and the voice of God answered him" (Exodus 19:19).

Theotimus, contemplation is an adoring, uncomplicated, and enduring attention of the soul to divine things. Little bees are called larvae. We really can't call them bees until they make honey. Prayer may be labeled "meditation" until it results in devotional honey. Then it may properly be called "contemplation." In the same way that bees fly across meadows collecting pollen, we meditate to stockpile the love of God. Once we have it, we begin to contemplate God. Our desire for

God leads us to meditate. An awareness of the loving presence of God results in contemplation. Our appetite is quickened rather than satisfied.

"When the Queen of Sheba heard about the fame of Solomon and his relation to the name of the Lord, she came to test him with hard questions. . . . Solomon answered all her questions; nothing was too hard for the king to explain to her. When the queen of Sheba saw all the wisdom of Solomon and the palace he had built, the food on his table, the seating of his officials, the attending servants in their robes, his cupbearers, and the burnt offerings he made at the temple of the Lord, she was overwhelmed. She said to the king, 'How happy your officials who continually stand before you and hear your wisdom!'" (1 Kings 10:1–8). Her meditation had changed to contemplation. She was spellbound. Sometimes we nibble a little food in order to gain an appetite. Once our appetite is excited, we dine with enthusiasm. Meditating upon God's goodness excites our desire to love God. With love in our hearts, we consider God's goodness in order to satisfy our need. Meditation is love's mother. Contemplation is love's daughter.

There is a continuing cycle. Because we find the object of our love beautiful, we love. Because we love, we enjoy the sight of our beloved. Love wants to dwell upon the beauty of the beloved, and the sight deepens devoted love. Which is the most powerful—love that makes us look or the sight that makes us love? We will never love what is unknown to us. Once knowledge results in love, love expands beyond the limitation of our knowledge. We can have more love for God than understanding of God. St. Thomas assures us it is possible for a simple person to be extraordinarily devout, while the cleverest of the educated are denied this gift. Love goes deeper than knowledge.

Brother Giles, a friend of St. Francis, once said to St. Bonaventure, "You educated people must be very happy. You understand so much about God. What can an idiot like me achieve?"

Bonaventure answered him, "It is enough to love God."

"There is no way an ignorant person can love God as well as one who is educated."

"That is not true. A poor, simple person may love God as much as a doctor of divinity." This thought enraptured St. Bonaventure.

Understanding assists the will in determining what is good. After the good is observed, understanding is not required for the practice of love. Knowledge of good generates love, but does not proportion it. We become angry when we learn of some injustice or injury. Unless our anger is controlled, it may well grow to greater intensity than the matter deserves. Emotions are not rational.

This effect is intensified in holy love. The intellect is not a participant. Faith is the guiding light. It assures us of God's infinite goodness. We find gold and silver by digging in the earth, hoping to discover some. We work hard without any positive knowledge that there is any precious metal where we are digging. If we find a little vein of the mineral we begin to dig more feverishly. Even a cold scent will excite a hound to hunt. This is the way it is, Theotimus, with faith.

Who would love light the most? Would it be the one born blind who has heard others philosophize about its beauty and value? Or would it be the farmer whose clear sight experiences the splendor of a sunrise? The blind person may have more actual knowledge of it, but the farmer harvests by it. This experience of fruition results in a lively and affective love. Intellectual knowledge can't do this. Actual experience of good is far more stimulating than a scientific analysis of it. Before children have tasted honey and sugar it is difficult to get them to eat it. Once they have tasted the sweetness, they enjoy them more than we wish they would, always eager to have some more.

Knowledge can be useful for the spiritual life. We are faithfully attracted by the object of our devotion, but understanding gives us a push. Pleasure draws us; knowledge pushes us. Knowledge is not a bad thing. It can greatly assist devotion. It is a pity that it can also be such a hindrance. "Knowledge puffs up, but love builds up" (1 Corinthians 8:1). There can be no doubt that the careful, systematized knowledge of such people as Cyprian, Augustine, Hilary, Chrysostom, Basil, Gregory, Bonaventure, and Thomas has improved their devotion even as their devotion has elevated their systematized knowledge.

MEDITATION AND CONTEMPLATION

Meditation examines the details. Contemplation considers the larger picture. Consider an ornate crown. You can study its precious jewels one by one, or you can see the harmony and rhythm of its overall design. Meditation sees the trees while contemplation sees the woods. While meditating we may think of God's mercy toward us and be led to love. In contemplation all the various elements and details come together in a unified and beautiful wholeness. In the Song of Songs the bride gives a detailed description of her sacred spouse: "His head is purest gold; his hair is wavy and black as a raven. His eyes are like doves by the water streams, washed in milk, mounted like jewels. His cheeks are like beds of spice yielding perfume. His lips are like lilies dripping with myrrh. His arms are rods of gold set with chrysolite. His body is like polished ivory decorated with sapphires. His legs are pillars of marble set on bases of pure gold" (Song 5:11–15). She extends this meditation on all the details until she finally gathers them into a single contemplation. "He is altogether lovely. This is my lover, this my friend" (Song 5:16).

Meditation is like smelling a dianthus, a rose, rosemary, thyme, and other things in the garden one at a time. Contemplation is comparable to smelling all of these things together in a potpourri. This mingled scent is deeper and far more complex than individual fragrances. Happy are the ones who have progressed beyond meditating upon the separate motives they have for loving God to a contemplation that unifies them all. This happened to St. Bernard. After he meditated upon every detail of the passion of Christ, he put it all together in a nosegay of adoring sorrow. With this he changed his meditation to contemplation, saying, "My lover is to me a sachet of myrrh" (Song 1:13).

This collective affection is far more powerful than all the individual affections that came before it. It is only one, but it contains the essence of all the others. It is contemplative affection. St. Augustine and St. Thomas tell us that in heaven our thoughts will not be scattered. One idea will contain them all. Water running near its source is in one stream. The closer we are to God, the more we contemplate in unity. This is what Jesus said of Mary. She "has chosen what is better, and it will not be taken away from her" (Luke 10:42).

Contemplation at its simplest has three approaches. We may focus on a single perfection of God, such as infinite goodness. We ignore other attributes during this time of contemplation. A bridegroom may be utterly distracted by nothing more than his bride's complexion. She may be beautiful in many other ways, but he is preoccupied with only one aspect.

A second possibility of contemplation is to give attention to several of God's attributes, but blending them together. We may not be able to describe anything in particular, but know that God is perfectly lovely. In this way the bridegroom may use a sweeping glance, head to toe, of his gorgeously attired bride. He perceives it all together, noticing few specific details. Her necklace, gown, and facial expression are lost on him. All he can think is that she is extremely attractive.

The third approach is to disregard divine perfections and give full attention to divine activity. We may contemplate the act of mercy in which our sins are forgiven, or the act of creation, or the raising of Lazarus from the dead, or the conversion of St. Paul. In the same way, the bridegroom may not single out the eyes, but only the sweet expression on his bride's face. He may not notice her lips, but might be touched by the words she speaks through them. "You are good, and what you do is good; teach me your decrees" (Psalm 119:68). "His mouth is sweetness itself; he is altogether lovely" (Song 5:16).

All three ways are valid. In each, contemplation is outstandingly delightful. We have approached the holy love of God and enjoy it. "I found the one my heart loves. I held him and would not let him go" (Song 3:4). This makes contemplation quite different from meditation, which nearly always takes a lot of effort on our part. Meditation is like eating. It is necessary to chew, turning spiritual meat this way and that between the teeth of consideration. Working on it, we grind it up to make it digestible. Contemplation is like drinking. There is no protracted labor by our teeth. We calmly swallow our drink with pleasure. There is even the possibility of sacred drunkenness. We can contemplate frequently and ardently enough to be completely out of ourselves and totally in God. This is quite different from inebriation of the flesh. It does not make us dull and stupid. Instead of lowering us to the level of animals, it lifts us to the level of angels. It allows us to live more in God than in ourselves.

To arrive at contemplation, we must hear the word of God, confer with others on spiritual matters, read, pray, sing, and conceive worthy thoughts. Since contemplation is the goal of these practices, we may call the ones who take this route contemplatives. Their occupation we may term a contemplative life.

DEEPER PRAYER

There are two levels of prayer in that state we call recollection. In one, those who are ready to pray, consciously place themselves in God's presence. During the time of prayer there is little concern with the external world or the business of life. Love inspires the prayer.

In the other, love does not inspire the prayer as much as it controls the prayer. It impels us, whether we wish it or not, to withdraw from the world and be as fully in God's presence as possible. It is not a matter of free choice on our part. It is not something we can seek whenever we please. It does not depend upon our participation. God makes it happen. St. Teresa of Avila says that the one who has described the prayer of recollection as a turtle drawing into its shell is correct with one exception. The turtle does this whenever it pleases, while a prayer of recollection is not our choice. It comes only when God is ready to do this for us.

Here is how it happens: it is completely natural for the soul to be drawn to unite itself with what it loves. Sometimes our Lord unnoticeably infuses into the deep places of our being a particularly delightful pleasantness that assures us he is present. This increases the ability of the soul to turn in toward its most interior part and be there with the friendliest and dearest of spouses. When bees are swarming they are ready to relocate far away, but they can be called to a hive prepared for them by gently tapping on a metal pan, or by the scent of honeyed wine or a mixture of herbs. It is the same when our Savior utters a word of love in secret or lets us feel his presence. He becomes the most desirable object of all and our souls are attracted to him.

"O God!" the soul cries out in the manner of St. Augustine. "I was looking for you everywhere, and you are within me." Mary Magdalene is looking frantically for Jesus all around the vicinity of the empty tomb. Her spirit is scattered until he speaks her name. At that moment, she collects her wits and throws herself at his feet. One word places her into recollection.

As soon as we recognize God is present, or that he is observing us from outside ourselves (even if we disregard his presence within us), our capacities come together out of respect for him. I know a woman who became even more conscious of the nearness of God when she heard a particular phrase. She would enter so deeply into herself that she seemed to be in a trance. Sometimes it would only last a moment; at other times it was more protracted.

The soul that is inwardly recollected in God's presence becomes so utterly distracted that its attention takes on a special quality. It is like being in a boat on a smoothly flowing river and not noticing any motion. This is what St. Teresa of Avila calls a quiet prayer. If I understand her correctly, this is only a step away from what she calls sleeping powers.

This spiritual tranquility is strong enough to shut down all awareness except the pleasure of enjoying the nearness of the one we love. It is a forgetting of self. It is like dozing in a light nap and barely hearing what our friends around us are saying.

During this time, the soul is enjoying a delicate awareness of the divine presence. It has no conscious enjoyment of it, but if one attempts to take it away or divert it, it will protest loudly. The soul will respond like a child that is waked up too soon from a nap. For this reason the heavenly shepherd begs the daughters of Jerusalem, "I charge you by the gazelles and by the does of the field: Do not arouse or awaken love until it so desires" (Song 2:7). Let it wake naturally. Theotimus, a soul that is recollected in God would not exchange that moment for the best this world has to offer.

Mary sits quietly at Jesus' feet listening to him speak. She is in profound tranquility. She neither weeps nor prays. Martha is busy, rushing back and forth. Mary does not notice her. What is Mary doing? Nothing, except listening. She is a container that is receiving every drop that comes to her. Martha attempts, as it were, to waken her. "'Lord, don't you care that my sister has left me to do the work by myself? Tell her to help me!' 'Martha, Martha,' the Lord answered, 'you are worried and upset about many things, but only one thing is needed. Mary has chosen what is better, and it will not be taken away from her'" (Luke

10:40–42). Mary's superior choice was to be peacefully quiet near Jesus.

The beloved St. John is usually painted in the Eastern manner at the Last Supper with his head on his Master's chest. He seems to be in deep repose, almost asleep. There is no chance that he could be dozing under those circumstances. It is a profound mystical sleep. He is like a baby who continues to nurse at his mother's breast even after falling asleep.

Have you ever noticed, Theotimus, how passionately hungry children will sometimes hold onto their mother's breast? They may begin nursing so eagerly that they cause their mother pain. After a while, the milk eases their urgency and begins to lull them to sleep. Still, they do not let go of the breast. Their lips continue to make a slow and gentle movement. They swallow with the slightest motion. They do this without thinking about it, but it brings them pleasure. If you remove such a child too soon from the breast the child will suddenly become wide awake and let out a howl of displeasure. It is not ready to be relieved of such contentment.

It is the same way with a soul that is at rest and quiet in God's presence. There are no perceptible physical sensations, no comments, and no visible activity. Only the highest part of the will is in motion. The divine presence is the ultimate satisfaction. Disturbing someone in this spiritual state is like taking a baby too soon from the breast. Since the Blessed Mother St. Teresa wrote that this was an excellent parallel, I do not hesitate to make good use of it.

If it should ever be that you find yourself in this simple, pure closeness with our Lord, stay there. Don't even attempt to think rational thoughts. This confident love, this devout sleep in the arms of the Savior, provides everything you need. It is better to be asleep on this sacred breast than to be wide awake anywhere else.

And why, Theotimus, should a soul recollected in God ever be disturbed? There is every good reason to continue in peace and repose. What else is there to find? "I found the one my heart loves. I held him and would not let him go" (Song 3:4). There is no need to be bothered with understanding. He is here with me. Reasoning is worthless. It is enough to feel his presence.

Some people are naturally active spiritually. They enjoy the experience and give a lot of attention to the progress they are making. Others need to examine and analyze their religious experience. They are like those who will not acknowledge they are rich unless they have an exact accounting of their money.

These approaches to prayer are actually hindrances. If God decides to grant them the sacred calm of his presence, they turn away from it in an effort to tabulate their personal response. Am I really content? Is this tranquility genuine tranquility? What is the degree of my quietness? Instead of being absorbed in the divine presence, they arouse their intellect to analyze their feelings. There is an enormous difference between being occupied with God, who is the source of our contentment, and being preoccupied with the contentment that God has given.

Don't be distracted, Theotimus, by yourself or the experience itself. If you give it too much attention it will be lost. Love it without loving it too restlessly. As a baby who turns its head away from the breast in order to study its feet will quickly return to it, so we must not be distracted for long wondering how our prayer is progressing. Quickly return to God's presence. There is no need to worry about the risks of losing this sacred calm by any activity of your body and mind that is neither frivolous nor indiscrete. St. Teresa assures us it is superstitious to be so careful that we fearfully refuse to cough or breathe. God does not withdraw his gift because of any involuntary actions.

Holy quiet exists in various degrees. Sometimes it is all the strength of the soul working in harmony with the will. Sometimes it is only in the will. At other times the soul is more than aware that God is present. It hears God speak. This speech does not consist in words, but in inward enlightenment and influence. The response is usually a respectful silence. There are also times when the soul speaks with God. This it does privately, delicately. It does not interrupt the holy quiet. Sometimes the soul neither hears nor speaks to its beloved. There is not even a perception that he has come to it. It is simply a matter of knowing that God is present and is pleased that it is there also.

What if St. John had actually fallen asleep on Jesus at the Last Supper? In this case, he would have been in his Master's presence without being aware of it. It takes more effort to place yourself in God's presence than to remain there. It requires conscious attention to achieve the former. Once we are in God's presence, we remain there by the strong ties of spiritual conversation and sharing. Actually, it is enough for us to simply stay where it pleases God for us to be. What a privilege!

Imagine a statue that has been placed in a niche. Suppose it could talk. You ask it what it is doing in that niche. It would answer, "Because my master put me here."

"But what is the point in sitting there doing nothing?"

"My master did not place me here to perform any task. It is enough that I am here."

"Poor statue," you reply, pressing the point, "what difference does it make that you are there?"

"I am not here for my own sake," it would answer. "I am here because it pleases my master. That is enough for me."

"But you don't see your master. How can you be content with pleasing him?"

"You are right. I can't see him. My eyes don't work any better than my feet. It satisfies me that my dear master is pleased to see me here."

You continue to debate with the statue and ask it, "But don't you at least have a desire to approach your master and offer him some greater service?"

"No. I have no desire to do anything other than what my master wishes."

"Then you have no desire to be anything other than an immovable statue in a hollow niche?"

The wise statue answers affirmatively. "I only desire to be a statue in this niche as long as it pleases my master. I am content to be here because the one who owns me is content to have me here. Because of him I am what I am."

It is good to remain in the presence of God. It is good to desire to be in God's presence. Even in our deepest sleep we can be profoundly in the holy presence of God. If we love God we sleep not only in his sight, but also at his pleasure. It is our Creator, our heavenly sculptor, who tucks us in bed even as statues are placed in niches. We settle down in God's presence as birds cuddle up in their nests. When we wake, if we think about it, we discover that God was constantly with us through the night. We were not separated from him in any way. Without observing anything at all, we can speak as Jacob did. "Surely the Lord is in this place and I was not aware of it" (Genesis 28:16).

This kind of quiet is truly outstanding because it does not have a trace of self-interest. The soul is not pondering contentment. The highest point of ecstatic love is not to be concerned with our own contentment, but God's.

THE LIQUEFACTION OF THE SOUL

Liquids take on the shape of whatever contains them. Lacking rigidity, they do not limit themselves to any particular form. Whether the container is round or square makes no difference. Liquids accept its shape and seek no other.

The human soul is not naturally like a liquid. It is shaped by habits and preferences. Our personal choices impose limits. When we speak of a stony or wooden heart, or a heart tough as iron, we refer to someone who does not easily receive divine influence. A gentle, pliable heart may be called a melting or liquefied heart. "My heart has turned to wax; it has melted away within me" (Psalm 22:14). The holy spouse in the Song of Songs said, "My heart had gone out to him [melted] when he spoke" (Song 5:6). It was no longer self-contained. It flowed out to its divine lover.

Balm is thick and syrupy. If stored for any length of time, it becomes even thicker and more solid. It can be dissolved and returned to a liquid state by heating it. Love acts like heat on the soul. Then there is a sharing together. Spirit mingles with spirit. "Your name is like perfume poured out" (Song 1:3). As the sun melts an exposed honeycomb, allowing the honey to flow out in the direction of the heat and light, so the soul flows toward what is loved. It goes beyond its natural limits.

Let me explain how this sacred outflowing of the soul occurs. An extraordinary desire to please God results in a kind of spiritual helplessness. The soul is no longer able to be self-centered. Like melted balm that has lost its firmness and solidity, the soul flows into what it loves. It is not a matter of impulsively clinging. Instead, there is a gentle, fluid movement into the greatly loved divinity. It happens in a way similar to the effect of a south wind on clouds. They melt and turn to rain, unable to contain themselves. The rain falls to the earth and saturates it, becoming one with it.

The soul, then, transcends its ordinary limits and flows toward God. It becomes mingled with God, absorbed and engulfed in God. After such an experience, there is little on earth that can provide contentment. St. Teresa of Avila said, "What is not God is nothing to me." This is the loving passion that incited St. Paul to say, "I no longer live, but Christ lives in me" (Galatians 2:20). "Your life is now hidden with Christ in God" (Colossians 3:3). An ordinary drop of water is thrown into an ocean of invaluable essence. If it could speak it would joyfully shout, "I continue to exist, but I do not live in myself. This great ocean lives in me. My life is hidden in this chasm."

Death is not the word to use to describe what happens to the soul that flows out to God. How can anything die that is being mingled with life? What changes is that the soul does not continue to live independently. Stars do not shine when the sun is in the sky, but they have not lost their light. They are simply overwhelmed by the brightness of the day. They are hidden in sunlight. The soul, being swallowed up in God, lives not to itself. God lives in the soul.

LOVE WOUNDS

If you barely love God, you will also hardly hate sin. Love is the primary source of all passions. It is love that arrives first. It penetrates deeply to the very foundation of the desire. Love wounds the heart.

Injuries hurt. Pomegranate juice is both sweet and sour. It is difficult to say which quality gives it such a delightful taste. It possesses a sweet tartness and a tart sweetness. Love is bittersweet. As long as we reside on earth the sweetness of love will never be perfectly sweet, and we will never be completely satisfied.

But how can the love of God bring injury and pain? If what one loves is absent, then, my dear Theotimus, the desire for it can be agonizing. Love can wound the heart with desire.

It would do little good to tell a child who has been stung by a bee that the source of such pain is also the source of sweet honey. He would reply, "Yes, I like honey, but this stinger hurts and as long as it remains in my cheek I am in misery. My face is swollen with it."

Love can produce pain. "My soul thirsts for God, for the living God. When can I go and meet with God? My tears have been my food day and night, while men say to me all day long, 'Where is your God?'" (Psalm 42:2–3). "Hope deferred makes the heart sick" (Proverbs 13:12).

There are different kinds of love pains. When love first disturbs us there is a crumbling of the solid stone of the heart. Portions of it flow out toward the beloved. This is tantamount to a wounding of the heart. Separating a portion of the heart from itself can be painful.

As noted above, desire always stings and wounds the heart.

In the case of heavenly love, there is a wound that is a gift from God. The allured soul has turned away from itself and flowed toward God, approaching as nearly as possible. Something holds it back. The soul's love is not the equal of the soul's desire. This is a miserable condition. There is a longing to fly, but the chains of this earthly life hold it down. It is beyond the soul's power to do anything about it. "Oh, that I had the wings of a dove! I would fly away and be at rest" (Psalm 55:6). The soul is torn by the tension that pulls in two directions. It can do nothing to achieve its great desire. "What a wretched man I am! Who will rescue me from this body of death?" (Romans 7:24).

In love with God, desperately desiring to love God more fully, the soul is not able to realize its ultimate goal. This is a dart in the side of a noble spirit. It hurts, but the pain is welcomed. Whoever desires strongly to love, also loves strongly to desire. Genuine misery would result from not desiring to love what is overwhelmingly worthy of love. Desiring to love brings pain. Loving to desire brings joy.

A bee dies after it stings. The Savior of our souls was fatally wounded by love for us, "even death on a cross!" (Philippians 2:8). We, then, are wounded for him. It is a wound of love. We are distressed by the slightest indication that God may not fully trust our love. Jesus asked Peter three times if he loved him. "Peter was hurt because Jesus asked him the third time, 'Do you love me?' He said, 'Lord, you know all things; you know that I love you'" (John 21:17).

The poor soul who would rather die than offend God and yet lacks even a spark of fervor, is badly wounded. Many have grown cold, become distracted, and feel the same reproach Peter felt. How can we say we love God when our soul is not enthusiastically with God? This is the dart of pain God hurls our way. It is sent with love. If we didn't love, we wouldn't worry that we might not love.

BRIEF BIOGRAPHIES
OF THE CONTRIBUTORS

SAINT AUGUSTINE
354–430

Augustine stands as one of the greatest and most influential of Christian theologians. "It may be safely predicted, that while the mind of man yearns for knowledge, and his heart seeks rest, the *Confessions* will retain that foremost place in the world's literature which it has secured by its sublime outpourings of devotion and profound philosophical spirit."[9]

It should be borne in mind that the *Confessions* was not intended to be an intellectual exercise, removed from the everyday realities of life. In it, Augustine seeks to lay bare his heart, his soul—before God and before his fellow men. It is an honest book and a book that speaks to the heart first of all.

We moderns may find some difficulty in his allegorizations, especially those found in the last three books. But one translator aptly remarked, "Where the strict use of history is not disregarded, (to use Augustine's expression), allegorizing, by way of spiritual meditation, may be profitable." Certainly his insights are not to be despised!

Born in 352, in the small city of Tagaste, Africa (in what is now Algeria), Augustine lived in the time of the growing ascendancy of the Christian Church and the growing decline of the Roman empire. It was scarcely a quarter of a century earlier that the great Council of Nicaea had been held, and there were heresies and schisms throughout the Christian world that still held sway over hearts and minds. Donatists continued to hold that many Catholic orders were invalid because they came through *traditori* (those who had denied the faith during the severe persecution and had later repented and been restored to the Church). In his later years Augustine would spend much effort in fighting for the unity of the Church against their schismatic beliefs. Arianism (denying the full divinity of Christ) succeeded in winning the allegiance of the Emperor and his mother, and echoes of that threat to the peace and unity of the Church continued to resound throughout Augustine's lifetime. But for Augustine personally, his sojourn among the Manicheans gave the background for much of the material we find in the *Confessions*. After his schooling under a harsh tutor in Tagaste, he was sent to Madaura for a time. Family finances forced his return home and resulted in an idle year, 369–70. He was then sent to Carthage, to what would be equivalent to a university, where he distinguished himself in the rhetorical school. His father died in 371, but his mother continued to support his schooling with the aid of a wealthy patron, Romanianus. It is evident that she continued to cherish high ambitions for his worldly success. While at Carthage, Augustine came under the influence of the Manicheans and took a mistress, to whom he was faithful for fifteen years. To them was born one son, Adeodatus.

After some years of teaching at Carthage, Augustine decided to go to Rome. His mother opposed the idea, but could not dissuade him. After a brief stay in Rome, he was appointed in 385 as Public Teacher of Rhetoric at Milan, where he first came under the influence of St. Ambrose. In 385–86, the Empress Justina demanded the surrender of two churches to the Arians. Ambrose led his people in a refusal to surrender the churches, even when confronted by military force. Augustine was aware of this crisis, but he was not personally involved.

Ten years spent with the Manicheans had brought Augustine many intellectual difficulties with their system. Although they had encouraged his own skeptical approach to the Holy Scriptures, they had not satisfied his thirst for sure knowledge nor his growing uneasiness with his disorderly life. With his mother's help, Augustine's mistress was dismissed and arrangements were made for his marriage, which had to be postponed because his intended was underage. But his struggles with the flesh resulted in his taking a new mistress, because he felt morally incapable of making a better choice. He chronicles the inner struggles which led, with timely help from Ambrose, to his departure from the Manicheans and his conversion to the Catholic faith. He was baptized at Easter, 387, along with his son, Adeodatus. Having resigned his position as professor of rhetoric, he and his company were waiting for a ship to make their way back to Africa when his mother suddenly became ill and died at Ostia, the port of Rome.

The next year, having returned to Tagaste and sold his property there, Augustine set up a monastic kind of community with a few friends, continuing his writing. In 391, with much misgiving on his part, he consented to be ordained presbyter at Hippo, a nearby city of about 30,000. The Church was not strong there, the city's population being a mixture of pagans, Jews, several schismatic sects, and a large group of Donatists. In 395 (in violation of the eighth canon of Nicaea) he was made assistant bishop to the aged Valerius, and succeeded him as bishop the following year.

It was not long after his election as bishop that he began the *Confessions*, completing them probably in 398. Thus they represent his thought and the account of his life in its midstream. He wrote this book "at the request of friends who begged him to commit to writing those recollections of his former life to which he often referred in private conversation. He consented for the characteristic reason that he desired his friends to mourn and rejoice along with him as they followed his retrospect of past years, and on his behalf to give thanks to God."[10]

Augustine's years as bishop involved struggles with errors he believed to be a threat to salvation and to the welfare of the Church on several fronts: Manicheans, Donatists, Arians, and Pelagians. In addition to these very real battles, the Roman Empire itself was under mortal assault. It is one of the great ironies of history that as Augustine finished his immortal *City of God* in the quiet of his monastic residence, the Vandals were pillaging the countryside of North Africa. "While the Vandals besieged Hippo, St. Augustine died (August 28, 410) in the sanctity and poverty in which he had lived for many years. Shortly afterward, the Vandals destroyed the city, but left his cathedral and library untouched."[11]

Sending the *Confessions* to a friend, Augustine wrote, "In these behold me, that you may not praise me beyond what I am. Believe what is said of me, not by others, but by myself."[4]

SAINT TERESA OF AVILA
1515–1582

Although there are several biographies of Teresa, she provides the details of her young life in her autobiography, *The Life of Saint Teresa of Avila By Herself.* We know from this writing that she loved and respected her father a great deal, that she and her brother were spiritually precocious youngsters who once ran away from home with the hopes of being martyred in Morocco, and that her mother died when she was fourteen. Teresa also provides a detailed overview of her journey from spiritual novitiate at an Augustinian convent, through several illnesses, to her attainment of perfect contemplation and her establishment of the Order of Discalced (Reformed, barefoot) Carmelites. Teresa also describes in visceral language the visions and raptures that accompanied her experience of inner contemplation.

On March 28, 1515, Teresa Sánchez de Cepeda y Ahumada was born to her father's second wife in the little Castilian town of Avila. Although her family was Christian, her grandfather, Juan Sánchez, of Toledo, was Jewish. She was educated as a young woman of her social rank. Teresa's mother taught her at home in the subjects with which she herself was familiar, but this did not include instruction in Latin or the religious classics. In addition to running away with her brother in hopes of attaining martyrdom, she often built little hermitages as a young girl.

When Teresa was fourteen, and her mother died, her reaction was to become enamored of chivalric romances and to immerse herself in worldly things. Her father sent her to a school run by Augustinian nuns when she was sixteen. When she was almost eighteen, Teresa became ill, and her father took her out of the school. Recovering from this illness, she experienced the first step on the way to becoming a Carmelite nun, for she read the letters of Jerome, the fourth-century monk who translated the Bible into Latin (the *Vulgate*) so that ordinary people could have access to it. After reading these letters, she decided to become a nun. At first, her father refused to let her join the convent, but he eventually consented, and, when she was twenty or twenty-one, Teresa entered the Carmelite convent of the Incarnation at Avila.

A year after entering the convent, Teresa became ill again. She experienced symptoms that in our time would be associated with an "anxiety attack." She was afflicted with violent attacks of vomiting, heart palpitations, cramps, and partial paralysis. Some interpreters have suspected that these problems were more mental than physical, for during this year Teresa was working hard to achieve perfect contemplation. Others have called Teresa's illness a malignant malaria. Whatever its cause, Teresa left the convent to be treated by her family doctors.

After three years she returned to the Carmelite convent, where she resumed her search for perfect contemplation. The convent itself was very large, with an estimated 140 nuns, and was somewhat relaxed in its adherence to and practice of its rules. Wealthy visitors from the town often visited the convent's parlor, and the nuns were free to leave the convent on a regular basis. During these years, Teresa first practiced the mental prayer that became the foundation of her own spiritual life and her teachings about prayer. Although she at first gave up this practice, she resumed it after her father's death in 1543, and did not give it up again. Between her entrance into the convent at twenty and her inner conversion in 1555 at age forty, Teresa writes that she was "engaged in strife and contention between converse with God and the society of the world."

When she was forty, she first read Augustine's *Confessions*. Though she had been educated briefly by Augustinian nuns as a young girl, she had not before been bathed in the waters of Augustine's piety. Her picking up of Augustine coincided with an inner conversion that had occurred as a result of her continuing practice of prayer. In her autobiography, she describes the effect that Augustine had upon her:

> O my Lord, I am amazed that my soul was so stubborn when you had helped me so much. I am frightened by how little I could do by myself and of those attachments that were obstacles to my determination to give myself entirely to God. When I began to read the *Confessions*, I saw myself portrayed there, and I began to commend myself frequently to that glorious saint. When I came to the tale of his conversion, and read how he heard the voice in the garden, it seemed as if the Lord had spoken to me. I felt this way in my heart. For some time, I was dissolved in tears, in great inward affliction and distress. The soul suffers so much, O Lord, when it loses its freedom. It was once its own mistress, but now it endures great torments. I am amazed today that I was ever able to live under such torture. May God, who gave me life to escape from such death, be praised.

After her conversion, Teresa became increasingly dissatisfied with the convent at Avila. Teresa was concerned mainly that the Avila convent did not encourage or honor solitude or poverty, two characteristics that she thought absolutely essential to the lives of those seeking perfect contemplation and union with God. Thus, around 1560, she sought to establish a religious community that would be governed by strict adherence to the rules of solitude and poverty. Although both civil and ecclesiastical authorities opposed her plan, she in 1562 founded the convent of St. Joseph of Avila, which became the model for at least sixteen other houses of the same type. There were thirteen nuns who took vows of poverty and solitude, and they were known by the coarse brown wool habits and leather sandals that they wore as they practiced their rule. The convent's income was provided by monetary offerings and by a program of manual work. The rules of the convent encouraged simple living, including abstinence from meat, and the convent building provided whatever essentials satisfied the basic needs of the sisters. Although Teresa thought of herself as a contemplative, she was as active as any other nun in caring for the convent, taking her turn at sweeping or other manual tasks. When she sought candidates for entrance into the convent, she looked for women who were intelligent and who had good judgment, for she thought that intelligent people could see their shortcomings and be taught ways to overcome them, while narrow-minded people are often so arrogant that they would never see their imperfections.

In the later half of the 1560s, Teresa's pupil John of the Cross pushed for a reform of Carmelite monasteries along the same lines that Teresa had pursued with her convent. These

Discalced Carmelite friars often provided spiritual direction to the nuns. Teresa died on October 4, 1582, in Alba de Tormes, as she returned from establishing a convent in Burgos. She was buried in Alba de Tormes. In 1622, she was canonized, and in 1970 she became the first woman saint to be declared a Doctor of the Church.

SAINT FRANCIS DE SALES
1567–1622

Francis de Sales became bishop of Geneva during the turbulent years of John Calvin's establishment there of the Reformed Church. His office had to be placed outside Geneva, across the French border at Annecy. His personality and demeanor were warm, courteous, and diplomatic, making him the ideal bishop in that volatile region. He was such a prolific writer that the works now collected at the religious community he founded (with Jane de Chantal) number twenty-seven volumes. Two titles stand out as extraordinary spiritual classics: *Introduction to the Devout Life* and *Treatise on the Love of God.*

Nine years of work preceded the publication of *Treatise on the Love of God* in 1616. The first edition of his *Introduction to the Devout Life* was produced in 1609 after the *Treatise* had already been in preparation for two years. His *Introduction* consisted of an edited collection of letters of spiritual guidance he had sent to Madame de Charmoisy, wife of the ambassador of the duke of Savoy. The easy-going style, combined with a depth of spiritual insight, made the book extremely popular. *Treatise on the Love of God* is a more carefully designed, systematic approach to a central Christian theme.

The book had its critics. It even generated open controversy. Fénelon and Bossuet snatched statements from its pages in a well-known scholarly debate. It has been pointed out that these respected religious scholars may not have fully understood what Francis de Sales was attempting to express. The same, of course, can be said of many other challenges to feebly under-stood Christian mystics such as Meister Eckhart.

Above all else, *Treatise on the Love of God* is the helping hand of a skilled spiritual director. De Sales is not interested in displaying his own elevated experiences with God. He wants to assure his readers that a deep and satisfying prayer life is not only possible, but also within the reach of anyone who agrees to accept what God is forever offering. He gives detailed instruc-tion on how to open the doors to such a prayer life, how to enter, and what to expect. He also is careful to point out the risks and misleading interpretations that are all too common. He then applies the most stratospheric union of the human soul with God to the living of commonplace, everyday life among others.

He tells us we may read some things in his *Treatise* that will not be easy to comprehend. This is inescapable. "I have written this for those who want to move beyond elementary spirituality. A more advanced discussion necessarily involves more obscure details."

⟞ NOTES ⟝

NOTES FOR PART I OF *The Confessions*
BOOK X

1. The *Confessions* changes focus at this point and becomes more philosophical and theological. Here we begin to hear the self-examination of the bishop of Hippo and his interpretation of the nature of knowledge and of creation itself.

2. From Romans 4:5. Augustine understands *justifico* in the sense of making actually just (righteous). He recognizes the possibility of interpreting the word in the sense of being reckoned just, but uniformly adopts the former interpretation.

3. This book has been called one of the most honest soul inventories extant from the ancient world.

4. The praying Christian is pictured as a thurible, a vessel for burning incense in the Temple [or in the Church]. Cf. Psalm 141:2: "Let my prayer be counted as incense before thee."

5. From Cicero: "After Anaximander came Anaximenes, who taught that the air is God." *On the Nature of the Gods.*

6. Plotinus said that to admire, to take as an object of pursuit anything different from one's own nature, is to acknowledge one's inferiority to it.

7. The Latin word is *anima*—physical life. Augustine sees animals as possessing the *interior sensus,* which correlates the data of sense perception but lacks *ratio*—the reason, which forms judgments.

8. Augustine here is very near the Platonic teaching that learning is remembering. In his *Retractions* (I, 8:2) he gave up this

opinion, saying rather that the mind has a natural affinity for the things of the intelligible world.

NOTES FOR THE BIOGRAPHY
OF ST. AUGUSTINE

9. Pilkington, Rev. J. C., Translator. *The Confessions of St. Augustine*, 1876.
10. Gibb, John and William Montgomery, Editors. *The Confessions of Augustine* [Latin Version], Introduction. Cambridge University Press, 1927.
11. *Ibid.*
12. Augustine. *Epistle ccxxi.*

ABOUT PARACLETE PRESS

WHO WE ARE

Paraclete Press is a publisher of books, recordings, and DVDs on Christian spirituality. Our publishing represents a full expression of Christian belief and practice—from Catholic to Evangelical, from Protestant to Orthodox.

We are the publishing arm of the Community of Jesus, an ecumenical monastic community in the Benedictine tradition. As such, we are uniquely positioned in the marketplace without connection to a large corporation and with informal relationships to many branches and denominations of faith.

WHAT WE ARE DOING

Books

Paraclete publishes books that show the richness and depth of what it means to be Christian. Although Benedictine spirituality is at the heart of all that we do, we publish books that reflect the Christian experience across many cultures, time periods, and houses of worship. We publish books that nourish the vibrant life of the church and its people—books about spiritual practice, formation, history, ideas, and customs.

We have several different series, including the best-selling Paraclete Essentials and Paraclete Giants series of classic texts in contemporary English; Voices from the Monastery—men and women monastics writing about living a spiritual life today; award-winning poetry; best-selling gift books for children on the occasions of baptism and first communion; and the Active Prayer Series that brings creativity and liveliness to any life of prayer.

Recordings

From Gregorian chant to contemporary American choral works, our music recordings celebrate sacred choral music through the centuries. Paraclete distributes the recordings of the internationally acclaimed choir Gloriæ Dei Cantores, praised for their "rapt and fathomless spiritual intensity" by *American Record Guide*, and the Gloriæ Dei Cantores Schola, which specializes in the study and performance of Gregorian chant. Paraclete is also the exclusive North American distributor of the recordings of the Monastic Choir of St. Peter's Abbey in Solesmes, France, long considered to be a leading authority on Gregorian chant.

Videos

Our videos offer spiritual help, healing, and biblical guidance for life issues: grief and loss, marriage, forgiveness, anger management, facing death, and spiritual formation.

Learn more about us at our website: www.paracletepress.com, or call us toll-free at 1-800-451-5006.

SCAN
TO
READ
MORE

You may also be interested in these Paraclete Essentials . . .

The Confessions of Saint Augustine
978-1-55725-695-9 | Trade paper, $16.99

The first autobiography ever written, Augustine's *Confessions* ranks among the most profound books in history. But it's more than that; this testament shows how God give rest to the weary and hope to the hopeless.

The Way of Perfection
978-1-55725-641-6 | Trade paper, $15.99

Millions have read and benefited from this book since it was first written nearly 500 years ago. St. Teresa's message of humility, simplicity, persistence, and faith is replete with language that it is at times earthy, and is full of self-deprecating humor.

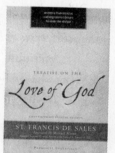

Treatise on the Love of God
978-1-55725-878-6 | Trade paper, $15.99

Francis de Sales's spiritual masterpiece was originally published in 1616 while he was bishop of Geneva. This contemporary English edition preserves St. Francis's gentle prose, enthusiasm for God, compassion, and good humor.

Available at bookstores everywhere.
PARACLETE PRESS   www.paracletepress.com   1-800-451-5006

You may also be interested in . . .

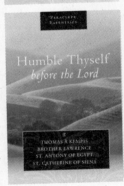